Continental Sports

Skills & Tactics of GYMNASTICS

ARCO PUBLISHING COMPANY, INC.
New York

Copyright © 1980 by Marshall Cavendish Limited

Published 1980 by Arco Publishing, Inc.
219 Park Avenue South, New York, N.Y. 10003

Printed in Hong Kong

Library of Congress Cataloging in Publication Data
  Skills & tactics of gymnastics.
  1. Gymnastics. I. Title.
GV461.A92 1980   796.4'1   79-18628
ISBN 0-668-04838-7

CONTENTS

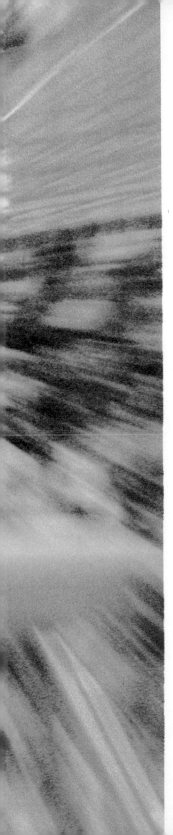

INTRODUCTION

To many gymnastics fans, the sport began in 1972. That was the year in which a teenage, gamine Soviet girl gymnast became one of the outstanding personalities of the Olympic Games in Munich. That girl was the unforgettable Olga Korbut. Her successes — and her failures — at Munich were seen by millions of viewers on television and a new era in sport had begun.

Olga captured the interest and imagination of young girls all over the world and the result was that gymnastics enjoyed a boom that has never been equalled by any other sport. Since 1972, the numbers of gymnasts and gymnastics clubs have increased at an incredible rate. For example, in Britain over three million badges have been issued in the training scheme set up for young gymnasts by the British Amateur Gymnastics Association and sponsored by *The Sunday Times*. The scheme, launched in 1971, gives young gymnasts four standards of gymnastics movements to achieve in succession. The response, since the impact of Olga Korbut, has been overwhelming.

What did Olga Korbut do to attract so many young people to gymnastics? First, she showed that gymnastics was a sport that used the natural movements of lively youngsters. Most children at some time like to run, turn somersaults, perform cartwheels and so on. Second, Olga demonstrated that gymnastics has a frisson of danger about it. In other words, it was a sport that was more than just a collection of simple exercises. Finally, she made it clear that gymnastics has a strong element of art in its presentation because a gymnast — particularly a girl gymnast — has to express herself with grace and style. All these ingredients, together with the personality of Olga, captivated young girls in millions.

Olga, surprisingly enough, was never a world nor an Olympic champion. It took a Romanian girl to show the world the nearest to gymnastics perfection. Nadia Comaneci did not seem to bring the sense of enjoyment to gymnastics that Olga Korbut did but she brought technical brilliance that has not yet been equalled. Nadia's first competition in the West was when she won the *Daily Mirror* Champions All in London in 1975. The virtually

Above: Nadia Comaneci of Romania proved to be the most technically perfect gymnast of the 1970s. She is the only gymnast to become European Champion three times in a row.

Right: When television brought Olga Korbut into the limelight at the 1972 Munich Olympic Games, gymnastics exploded into a boom sport.

unknown Romanian then went on to win the European Championships later that year and the overall Olympic title in Montreal in 1976. Amazingly, Nadia achieved a perfect score — 10 — seven times. Now there was another star to boost the sport.

But gymnastics did not begin with Olga and Nadia. Its history can be traced back to ancient times and ancient civilizations — those of the Chinese, Indians, Persians, Greeks and Romans. The Greeks and Romans in particular set high store by physical culture but when their empires passed away, so did gymnastics in the form in which it was practised. It was up to acrobats and dancers for many successive centuries to perform movements similar to some parts of the sport as it is known today. For example, tumbling has passed down the ages as an entertainment.

In the eighteenth and nineteenth centuries, the importance of physical exercise began to attract the attention of educationalists in Denmark, Germany and Sweden and so once more, in various forms, gymnastics became popular. Physical fitness developed through

Below left: Gymnastics has its roots in the games and sports of many past civilizations. This vase from Ancient Greece shows an acrobat performing.

Above: Balancing acts in many forms have long been popular entertainment, as this picture of the Forum in Ancient Rome demonstrates.

Right: There is a familiar look about the acrobatics portrayed in these seventeenth century German prints.

gymnastics was considered by many people to be vital in military training. A leading pioneer was Ludwig Jahn (1778-1839) of Germany who established many *turnverein* (gymnastics clubs) and developed such equipment as the rings, parallel bars, horizontal bar and the horse. The first gymnastics club in the United States was started in 1850, while the Amateur Gymnastics Association (now the British Amateur Gymnastics Association) was formed in 1888.

The enthusiasm for fitness in the nineteenth century, together with the growth of several sports, led to the founding of the first modern Olympic Games. These were held in Athens in 1896 and gymnastics was one of the seven sports included. It has been an Olympic sport ever since. Women's gymnastics were introduced to the Olympic Games in 1928 and subsequently developed into its four disciplines of vault, asymmetric bars, balance beam and floorwork which were much more suited to femininity than the strength pieces of men's gymnastics. Since 1952, women from the Soviet Union have dominated the Olympic Games. Among the most famous Soviet women stars of the last two decades have been Larissa Latynina and Ludmila Tourischeva. In 1968, however, a Czech gymnast, Vera Caslavska, won four gold medals at the Mexico Olympic Games.

Below: Ludmila Tourischeva of the Soviet Union was one of the great gymnasts of recent years. She achieved the top overall titles in the world – Olympic, World, World Cup and European. Ludmila is now a coach to a future generation of Soviet stars.

Above: The forerunner of the balance beam? An eighteenth-century print from France shows tightrope walkers entertaining a crowd – but aided by balance poles.

Opposite (below): Gymnastics was included in the first post-War Olympic Games in London in 1948. It took the next Games, at Helsinki in 1952 when the Soviet Union participated for the first time, to shape women's gymnastics into its present form.

The International Federation of Gymnastics (FIG) was founded in 1881 with three member countries. Today, seventy-five countries belong to the FIG. Since 1950, the World Championships organized by the FIG, have been held every four years. From 1979, The World Championships take place in the year preceding the Olympic Games and is used as a qualifying tournament for the Games. In 1975 the World Cup was established and now takes place every year. There are many important regional competitions, too, such as the Pan-American Games and European Championships.

Every member country of the FIG has a national federation which controls gymnastics through local member organizations. Most federations appoint national coaches who are responsible for keeping standards high and for selecting and training national teams. The basic unit in every federation is the school or neighbourhood gymnastics club from which every first-class gymnast starts on her career. The world-wide boom in gymnastics has meant, however, that in many countries there are too few coaches.

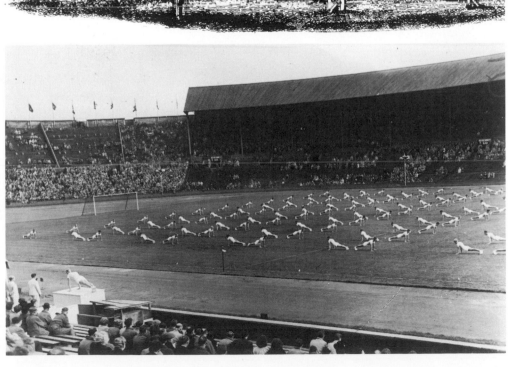

Most leading gymnasts have been encouraged in the sport at school. Gymnastics is now very popular with primary schools because it is not only a year-round activity but can also involve boys and girls. Basic gymnastics can be practised in assembly halls or gymnasiums and with equipment which many schools already have.

The greatest boost to modern gymnastics is undoubtedly television. The medium is ideal for the sport and is able to capture its visual qualities and project them to a world-wide audience. Television coverage of gymnastics on a universal scale began with the Olympic Games of 1960 in Rome, and since then, most of the world's most important gymnastics events have been televised and presented in some form to television audiences everywhere.

This book will tell you how to approach gymnastics if you are determined to reach the top. It does not offer you an easy formula for success. Nor can it explain and illustrate all the many moves that make up modern gymnastics. But it can introduce you to most of the elements you must master to become a competent gymnast. As with every other sport, to succeed you will need other qualities such as determination, good coaching and a great deal of natural ability.

If nothing else, this book will help you to understand something of an exciting sport which has moved from a minor position to a major place in physical culture in a few years. And, as you know, the more you understand it, the more you will enjoy it.

Below: Gymnastics owes its present popularity to television. A landmark was the first world-wide TV coverage of the sport at the 1960 Rome Olympic Games.

Opposite: Elena Davydova is one of many Soviet gymnasts who have captivated world audiences in the last decade.

CHAPTER 1

PREPARING FOR GYMNASTICS

Thorough preparation is the key to success in gymnastics, not least because of the combination of different skills the sport requires.

How did you become interested in gymnastics? Many people's interest was aroused by watching some of the world's best gymnasts perform on television; gymnasts such as Olga Korbut, Ludmila Tourischeva, Nadia Comaneci and Nelli Kim. Others may have been to a tournament, international match or display at which famous stars appeared. Wherever you have seen top-class gymnastics performed, you will, like millions of girls all over the world, have been attracted by the grace, skill and daring of the gymnasts.

Opposite: Some of the physical qualities required by a top gymnast.

You may already be a member of a gym club, either at one run at school or at one established in your home area. If so, you will know something of the ways by which gymnasts learn to master their sport. Like most keen gymnasts, you probably find that the training sessions at your club are lively and enjoyable. Most clubs have two sections: one for gymnasts who attend just for recreation, relaxation and enjoyment and the other for gymnasts with talent or who show signs of being able to become successful competitive gymnasts. If you belong to this second group of elite gymnasts and you, too, really want to succeed in gymnastics, there are four vital points which must be understood before serious training begins.

1. **It takes a long time to become a good gymnast.** Every star you see performing worked for years to get where she is. Thus gymnastics is a sport which requires endless patience and hard work.
2. **Gymnastics is a sport of individual performances.** In gymnastics, you are never seen to win a race or score points off an opponent. This means that you are not competing so much against other gymnasts as against yourself. The sweetest success for every gymnast is mastering the moves that must be learned to make progress.
3. **Your body must be in peak condition.** This goes for almost every sport but gymnastics makes particularly strenuous demands on the human frame. Therefore you must take good care of your body to achieve the best results.
4. **The best gymnasts are those who have learned gymnastics step by step.** When you are beginning gymnastics, it is very tempting to pay little attention to the basic skills and physical preparation and go for learning advanced moves and routines instead. The result will be that your exercises will receive low marks because you perform them without the finishing touches of style, mobility and expression. Remember the old saying: don't run before you can walk. To sum up, if you want to get to the top in gymnastics, you must spend time preparing your body and acquiring basic skills. Only then will you achieve success. But before you go into the gymnasium,

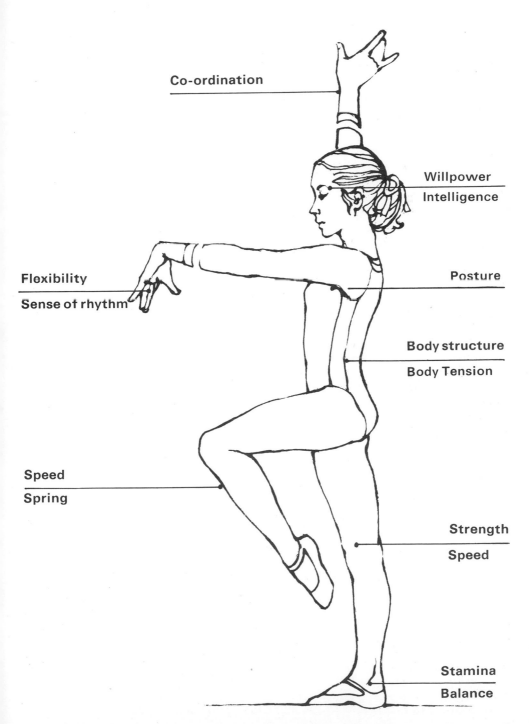

Co-ordination

Willpower
Intelligence

Flexibility
Sense of rhythm

Posture

Body structure
Body Tension

Speed
Spring

Strength
Speed

Stamina
Balance

19

Below: The career of the average gymnast starts when she is about eight years old and finishes when she is about 20. However, some gymnasts start as early as five years old and others are still competing well into their 20s

you must learn about some factors that affect every gymnast. What makes a good gymnast? What raw material do leading coaches look for when they select girls for advanced training?

Ideally, gymnastics should be taken up between the ages of eight and ten. During this period, you should concentrate on learning basic skills. From ten to thirteen years, you will be linking these skills to form complete exercises and later you will be ready to learn the more difficult movements. As a matter of interest, scientists have found out that girls reach their greatest strength

8–10   **10–13**   **13–15**   **15–20**

potential when they are between fifteen and nineteen years old. So in fact a talented gymnast can reach peak form at the age of fourteen to sixteen. As you may remember, Nadia Comaneci was fifteen when she won the overall title at the Montreal Olympic Games in 1976.

To become a good gymnast, then, you must have certain abilities which are part physical, part mental. Recently, some Soviet gymnastics experts made a list of qualities, in order of importance, required by the perfect gymnast. While very few people can call themselves 'ideal gymnasts', the list provides useful guidelines for any

Below: Nadia Comaneci became overall Olympic Champion when she was 15. This was at the 1976 Montreal Games.

gymnast who wants to understand what it means to aim for the top in gymnastics. The physical qualities, and many of them can be improved through exercises, are:

Strength. You must have strength throughout your body in the muscles of your arms, upper arms and wrists, legs, stomach, back and shoulders. Strength helps you perform your exercises without strain.

Stamina. You must be able to keep working without getting too tired. A top gymnast may have to train at least ten hours a week as well as taking part in competitions.

Co-ordination. This is a natural ability of combining movements of your limbs such as arms, trunk and legs. You will need this ability to link several skills together. You will also need a sense of timing.

Body structure. A gymnast of the right proportions will find it easier to make progress than one who lacks certain characteristics. For example, excess body weight will make harder work for your muscles. The ideal gymnast should have long fingers and arms with short legs and torso.

Flexibility. Suppleness in all joints — legs, back and particularly in the hip and shoulder regions — is essential to achieve the maximum possible range of movement.

Below and opposite: Some gymnasts find that they already possess essential physical qualities. Others may have to train hard to acquire them. All will have to combine them when learning movements.

Strength

Stamina

Co-ordination

Flexibility

23

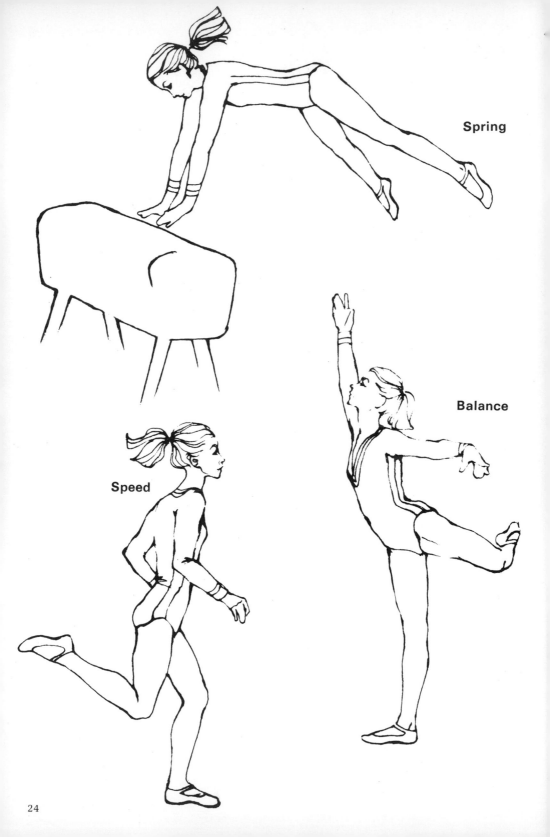

Spring

Balance

Speed

24

Spring. Being able to leap well is an essential part of many gymnastics movements. So your legs must have the power to lift you high.

Skill. Skill is part natural talent, part the ability to learn the essentials of a gymnastics movement very quickly and to perform it in the most confident way possible. Many famous gymnasts show this quality very early on in their gymnastics career.

Speed. A gymnast must be able to run quickly. This is essential for the vault and some tumbling moves.

Balance. No gymnast succeeds without ability to balance. Nowhere is this more apparent than on the balance beam where you have to perform on a platform not wider than four inches.

Sense of rhythm. You must, of course, be able to walk and run in time to music because floorwork is performed to music.

If these are the physical abilities which go towards making a top-class gymnast, what are the mental ones? Here they are, again in order of importance as the Soviet experts see them:

Willpower. Willpower covers determination, self-discipline, bravery and confidence. You may say that these qualities are connected. As we have seen, gymnastics calls for long, hard exhausting work, and for success, a gymnast must be prepared to undergo many pressures. A will to succeed, courage to tackle new and difficult skills and confidence in the outcome must go together with physical progress. As John Atkinson, National Staff Coach

Opposite and below: The successful performance of difficult routines depends on mastering many skills requiring thorough physical preparation.

Balance

Sense of rhythm

to the British Amateur Gymnastics Association, says: 'Talent alone is not enough when it comes to achieving really high standards.'

Intelligence. As a gymnast, you must be a clear, quick thinker, ready to co-operate in learning and mastering new moves and routines. You must also be able to adapt immediately to any mishaps in a routine during competition.

Expressiveness. Gymnastics, being a sport allied to art, has a creative element that calls for poise, imagination and elegance in its performance. A thoughtful gymnast will realize that, like a ballet dancer, she must convey mood and feeling to her audience by her movements. She must also show amplitude, a term meaning that every movement must be taken to its fullest and furthest point of stretch.

Emotional stability. A gymnast's life can be full of pain and frustration, triumphs and disappointments. You must have the self-discipline to come through times of stress without letting the occasions affect your temperament or your aim to be the best. Included here is the ability to accept strong criticism without getting upset and being able to work confidently without relying on encouragement too much.

If you belong to a gym club, you will obviously have many of these qualities. Others you can try to develop while you seek to improve your skills. But remember again that the way to the top in gymnastics depends on physical preparation combined with learning basic skills. That way, you will enjoy your sport even more.

Two other elements of a gymnast's make-up are:
Posture. An essential part of preparing for gymnastics is making sure that your posture is correct. You must know how to stand well and walk well. How well do you stand? Does your stomach stick out? Does your seat or do your knees stick out? Try and stand with your head held up and your shoulders back and relaxed and down. Keep your seat and stomach in and your feet straight. When you walk, try and do so with the same elegance and poise. Good posture not only creates a favourable impression with judges and audiences but also is necessary for balance and control throughout training and performances. Simple ballet exercises will help.

Body tension. A trained gymnast can control and tighten muscles in regions of her body so that they do not give way during an exercise. This is known as achieving body tension. The muscles most concerned are those in your stomach, back, seat and legs. You should practise tightening and relaxing these muscles as part of your training.

If preparing your body for gymnastics is vital, so is caring for your body. You must keep your skin clean; bacteria form if sweat is allowed to remain on your skin for long and this can produce sweat rash. So bathe or shower after a training session or competition and use soap. Take care of your hands; they are of fundamental importance in gymnastics. Keep them moist with hand lotion two or three times a day but never before practice. Nails should be kept short. It will help you to have hair that does not cover the eyes and which can be kept neat

Above: As well as being supple and strong, a gymnast must acquire a reliable sense of balance.

without too much attention. It must be tied back if you wear it long. Like all athletes, you should be aware of the value of getting a full night's sleep and of being a non-smoker. Do not train if you do not feel well, particularly if you feel feverish.

One important way for a gymnast to feel fitter and improve her performances is to know something about the food she eats and the science of nutrition. If you neglect your diet, your performance can be affected by deficiency in certain vitamins and minerals, lack of energy and weight problems. Good nutrition depends on your body having an adequate supply of nutrients, the components of food vital for health and well-being. Nutrients are classified as proteins, fats, carbohydrates, vitamins, minerals and water. As a gymnast, you will use a great deal of energy — just the same as a footballer. The energy that food provides is measured by calories. According to Scilla Miller, an expert on nutrition, a girl weighing fifty kilos (110 lbs) will need about 2000 calories in a normal day. If she takes part in gymnastics for just one hour, she will need an additional 480 calories. If she has not eaten sufficient calories, she will have insufficient energy and will lose weight.

The main nutrients supplying energy are carbohydrates, proteins and fats, carbohydrates being the main source. Carbohydrates are the starches and sugars found in foods such as fruits, breads, vegetables, cakes and biscuits. Fats are plentiful in cheese, cream, butter, salad oils, bacon and nuts. Protein is supplied by meat, fish, milk, cheese, nuts and eggs and you should eat at least three of these foods a day. Protein is also the chief tissue builder and needed to repair and replace body tissue. Some nutritionists recommend that too much animal protein and fat should not be eaten.

In a good well-balanced diet, there should be no need for vitamin or mineral supplements but you should make sure of taking Vitamin C daily through fruits and salad foods. Otherwise, take multi-vitamin and mineral tablets. Drink plenty of liquids, too.

Some teenage girls feel tired, dizzy and have frequent headaches, leading to lower standards of performance. This could be deficiency in iron. Iron can be obtained from spinach, eggs, kidneys, liver and meat or in iron tablets prescribed by a doctor.

So do not let your eating habits hinder you from becoming a good gymnast. Two points to remember are: do not eat too much food or else you will clearly put on weight, and make sure that you always have a good breakfast. Research has shown that breakfast eaters are more alert and productive in the morning and more resistant to tiredness during the day than those who go without breakfast.

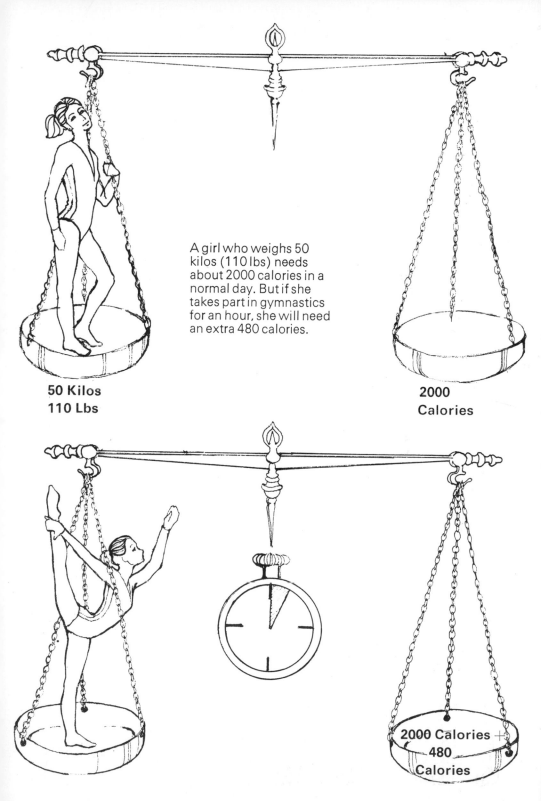

A girl who weighs 50 kilos (110 lbs) needs about 2000 calories in a normal day. But if she takes part in gymnastics for an hour, she will need an extra 480 calories.

50 Kilos
110 Lbs

2000
Calories

2000 Calories +
480
Calories

Keep-fit exercises for home

Exercising at home will not only keep you fit but also will help your physical preparation for gymnastics when you are not in a gymnasium. Here are some exercises which will help tone up all parts of your body. You need only spend a few minutes a day on them.

Running. Running is one of the simplest exercises of all. It uses most of your muscles and helps to give you stamina. Half a mile a day is ample.

Balance and posture. This exercise for the legs will help improve balance and posture. Just skip on the spot and raise your knees in turn as high as possible. Then see how long you can stand on the toes of one foot while holding the other knee up high.

Arms: swing. Stand with your feet slightly apart with your arms by your sides. Then raise your arms forward in line with your shoulders. Then, keeping them straight, swing them down and then up quickly in front of you to stretch above your head. Repeat several times.

Below: Daily exercises should involve every muscle. Strenous exercises however should not be undertaken until the body is warm.

Arms: strength. Lie on your stomach with your legs straight and toes pointed. Place your hands under your shoulders, press, and raise your body, keeping your knees and feet on the floor. Do this slowly. Lower your body and repeat before your chest touches the floor.

Shoulders. Standing straight with your feet apart, put your hands behind your seat with the palms together, keeping your arms straight. Then swing your arms sideways, still keeping them straight, to clap your hands high above your head. Then swing your arms down and clap them behind your seat. Repeat several times.

Stomach. Lie on your back with your arms stretched above your head. Raise each leg in turn off the floor to a height of 1 ft and hold for a short time. Then raise both legs together.

Waist. Stand with your feet apart. Reach over your head with your left arm towards your right side. Then slide your right arm down the side of your right leg as far as you can reach for six or seven times. Then repeat.

Below: There are many other exercises which you can perform. If you are in regular training, ask the advice of your coach, teacher or gymnastics club.

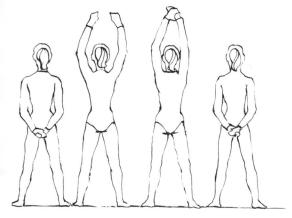

Body tension. Lie on the floor with your hands on a bench or side of a bed. Then, raise your body, keeping your feet on the floor. The aim is to get your body in a straight line from your hands to your feet.

Poise. Walk around with a book on your head. This will help you to stand and walk straight. There are other ways of learning about gymnastics at home too. Here are some ideas.

1. Become a member of your country's gymnastics federation. That way, you will learn about big national events and competitions.

2. Subscribe to gymnastics magazines. They provide up-to-date news as well as supplying interesting articles about training, gymnastics personalities and major international events.

3. Keep a scrapbook for useful pictures and newspaper clippings about gymnastics.

4. Get a notebook to write down any interesting facts that you may learn about the sport.

5. Try and watch top-class gymnastics. If you have the chance, go to any big event where advanced gymnastics is being performed. Or, look out for gymnastics events on television when they are presented by sports programmes.

6. Read books about gymnastics.

The next stage is to move into the gymnasium and see how you can tackle physical conditioning and learning essential skills.

Opposite: Elfie Schlegel of Canada won the overall title at the 1978 Commonwealth Games in Edmonton.

Below: See if you can persuade a friend or member of your family to exercise regularly with you.

CHAPTER 2

IN THE GYMNASIUM

Although gymnastics is a sport for individuals, a gymnast will spend most of her time in club training sessions in the gymnasium.

This section is for the conscientious gymnast who wants to do her best for herself and her club, and who has her sights set high.

Gym clubs today function in a great variety of places. Some are in modern sports centres. Others are in old converted buildings — sometimes even churches or warehouses. Many clubs are based in schools and others have to operate wherever they can find the space. Wherever your club is based, try and be a conscientious club member and co-operate as much as possible. Arrive for training and competitions on time. Help to take out and put away equipment. Be tidy in appearance and behaviour. Join in events that help to raise funds to buy equipment for the club, and always be prepared to learn about gymnastics from coaches and more experienced gymnasts.

It is through your club that you will receive the basic training to become a competent gymnast and that is why it is important to give as much to the club as you get out of it. The aim of this section is to give you hints to enable you to work at gymnastics in the club gym with as much confidence as possible. Some things will be obvious, others you will find are based on experience, and more will become apparent as progress is made. All of them will help make training more rewarding.

Clothing

For the most important items of dress, the club will probably have made some arrangement with a supplier. In general, though, all gymnastics clothing should fit well and be light. Some clubs allow their gymnasts to train in informal clothing such as sweaters and tights and here the same principle should be observed.

You should wear nothing loose that will get in the way as you perform movements, or anything dangerous such as buckle fasteners. All the clothing you wear for gymnastics should be kept clean, too, as this creates a favourable impression when you perform, and gives you confidence.

Track Suit. A track suit is a very good investment. Not only does it keep you warm but it also protects the skin from scrapes and abrasions during training. A well-fitting track suit can look very smart, too. Your club will probably have its own distinctive track suit which can be ordered when you join. Some clothing of this kind is necessary, particularly for warm-ups.

Leotard. As you will know, a leotard is essential for gymnastics. When you order this one-piece item, make sure that if fits really well. A leotard which is too tight or too loose-fitting looks most unattractive. At the same time, it must allow complete freedom of movement. Your club will have its own leotard for performances and displays and it is a good idea to order at least two so that you can have one spare.

Opposite: Track suits and leotards are clothing which every aspiring gymnast needs. Many clubs order them to their own design. Gymnasts should not practice on apparatus without adequate supervision.

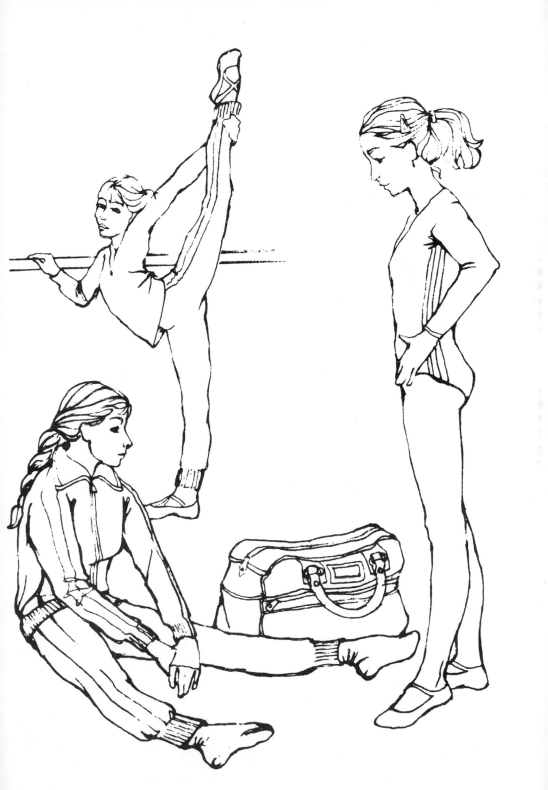

Above: Shoes and handguards must not only be comfortable but safe. They must never become worn nor slippery.

Shoes. There are many kinds of gymnastics shoes or slippers. These should be worn in preference to socks or bare feet when there is a risk of slipping or being injured. Socks should not be worn with slippers either, because they can make a gymnast look untidy. Gymnastics slippers should be light and fit securely, with light soles. Remember not to let the soles become too worn and slippery, or your slippers could let you down with a real, and very painful, bump.

Handguards. You will need a reliable pair of handguards for performing on the asymmetric bars. As their name implies, they guard the palms of the hands from friction caused as you swing on the bars. Handguards are made of leather, lamp wick or synthetic materials. They must fit comfortably and tightly. When you try them on, place the two middle fingers in the holes and buckle the straps around your wrists. Because your hands have to grasp the bars, the handguards must fit snugly when the hands are cupped slightly. The smooth side of the handguards should lie on your palms so that the bars can be gripped with the rough side. It is important to check handguards regularly for wear. Make sure that the rough surface does not become too smooth so that your hands lose their grip. Do not use handguards if they are torn or if the stitching needs repair.

Hold-all. A very convenient item to have in the gym is a hold-all or duffle bag for your clothing and possessions. Try and obtain one which can be locked for security.

Learning aids

In your hold-all, keep a training notebook and pencil for recording any hints or training programmes given to you by your coach, or any good ideas that you come across during training sessions. Many gymnasts keep a spare music tape or cassette handy as this is useful for practising floor exercises. Another useful item to have in the gym is your own white, plastic-covered square tile, measuring, say, 150 × 150 × 1mm thick. On this square you can draw diagrams with felt tipped pens or magic markers and so use it to plot floor exercises. The diagrams can be changed or wiped off without difficulty.

Many gym clubs keep progress cards which show how their members are developing as gymnasts. You can do much the same by recording your own progress in a diary. You should write down each skill as you master it, and details of awards or achievements in training schemes or competitions. You will find it interesting, too, to make a note of when you train and for how long.

If you are fortunate, you may have a chance to see yourself performing on videotape. More and more clubs are investing in this playback medium because their members can then see and evaluate themselves when they tackle difficult moves. Coaches can stop the tape at any given point to show the gymnasts where execution needs correcting.

Below: A very useful item for gymnasts is a white, plastic covered square on which floor exercises can be drawn with magic markers. The diagrams can be changed or wiped off without difficulty.

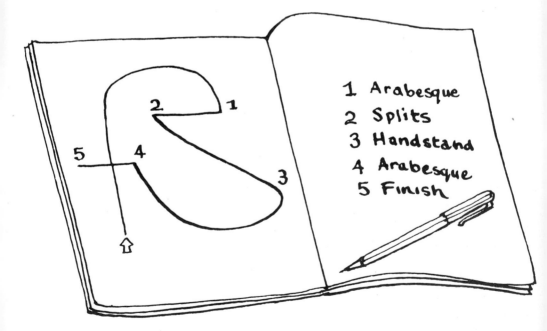

1 Arabesque
2 Splits
3 Handstand
4 Arabesque
5 Finish

Your coach

While you should always collect as much information as you can about gymnastics, you will learn most about your sport from your coach. In every club the number of coaches compared to the number of gymnasts varies: you may be coached as a member of a large group of gymnasts by just one coach. Really promising youngsters are sometimes able to have a coach all to themselves.

However you are coached, remember that the coach will be qualified and therefore have a great deal of experience in gymnastics. It is very much in your interest, therefore, to pay attention to and respect what your coach tells you. It may be a comment on a move, or an explanation of an exercise or an idea for a new element in a routine, but whatever it is you owe it to your coach to watch, listen and then experiment carefully. It is unfair on you, your fellow-gymnasts and your coach to waste time. A good coach will try and understand what kind of person as well as a gymnast you are so that he or she can help you perform your best in training or in competitions. This help will include drills, warm-up exercises and specific conditioning programmes for strength, flexibility and stamina.

Every gymnast should try and understand her coach. Do what he or she suggests and if you have any problems at all, speak up. You may have several coaches during your gymnastiscs career. Whoever they are, co-operate with them, because you cannot reach the top — and stay there — without their help.

Above: Romanian coach Bela Karoly not only discovered Nadia Comaneci when she was a little girl but also trained her into a world-class gymnast.
The influence of a coach can make all the difference to a gymnast's career.

The warm-up

A cardinal rule of gymnastics is that before starting any training or competition you must warm up your body. Serious accidents could occur if movements are tackled with 'cold' muscles, so the aim of the warm-up is to exercise all the joints so that the muscles are relaxed and stretched. At the end of the warm-up, specific exercises can be performed for suppling and strengthening. The body will warm up more quickly if warm clothing such as a sweater, track suit, or tights, is worn especially when you are training in a warm building. In its simplest form the warm-up period should last between twenty and thirty minutes. There are many suitable exercises for warming up and your coach or gym club will teach you some. Here are some suggestions of exercises for you to follow, in turn, which will warm you sufficiently at the start of a training session.

1. Start off gently by walking around the gym.
2. Then run on your toes, raising your knees.
3. Vary your running by skipping, side-stepping or making small leaps in the air.
4. Now stop running and exercise your shoulders. You

Below: Every gymnast must warm up for at least 20 minutes before training.

can do this by swinging your arms in different directions or circling them.

5. Then circle your hips — as with a hula hoop.

6. Sit, legs straight in front, and stretch the toes backwards and forwards.

7. Kneel and arch the body back. Then fling the arms up and backwards. Repeat.

8. Stretch your arms forward and above your head, hands back to back, fingers interlocked.

9. Stand and lunge quickly from side to side with your hands above your head.

After this, the body will be warm enough to try suppling exercises. Here are some examples of suppling exercises which will help you prepare for the harder skills in gymnastics.

1. Sit on the floor with legs straight and wide apart with toes pointed. Stretch forward with your arms and try and get your stomach on the floor (for legs and hips).

2. Sit with your legs straight in front of you and the back straight, too, and pull your body towards your toes (for hamstrings).

Below: Once your body is warmed up, you can move on to suppling exercises.

Above and opposite: It may take time to achieve the splits positions, but regular exercising will help.

3. Stand with your legs straight and together. Reach down, keeping your legs straight, to touch the floor beside your feet. Try and touch with your palms, hands facing backwards (for the hips).

4. Lie on your back with your knees bent and hands flat on the floor beside your head. Push up into a 'bridge' position (for shoulders and back).

5. Splits: with one leg bent and the other straight on the floor behind, bounce up and down. Increase the distance between your feet, ie move the front foot forward, until you move into the splits position. Then change around, with the other leg forward. For side splits, perform the same exercise with the legs astride. Your straight leg in either position must be kept stretched.

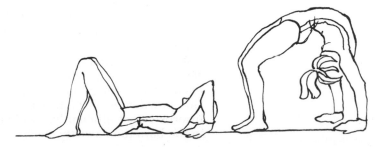

Training schemes and programmes

Can all the hard work which goes into training have an immediate purpose? Yes, it can. Most countries run national gymnastics programmes for girls at different levels. In Britain, the programmes are administered through the British Amateur Gymnastics Association (BAGA), the governing body of the sport in Britain. The basic programme for clubs and schools is the *Sunday Times/BAGA* Awards Scheme in which young gymnasts work towards four awards. A more advanced awards programme is the Gold Top Milk Scheme which leads girls on to apparatus training. The major British scheme is the National Development Plan for Girls which can take a serious participant through seven grades up to the British Championships. Schemes such as these give more than an incentive. They also give grounding in basic movements and routines which help your development as a gymnast. Each scheme has booklets or posters which show the movements or routines which have to be learned. If you, through your club or school, are involved in a national or, indeed, a regional training programme, make sure that you understand how the programme works. It is always more rewarding to train with a real objective in mind. Your club or your coach will help you decide when you are ready to enter an advanced training programme which may or may not end in a competition.

Safety

Because gymnastics has a strong element of danger in it, especially on apparatus such as the asymmetric bars, it is essential that everyone training or competing in the sport is aware of the need to observe safety rules. Safety is largely a matter of common sense; however, many gymnasts — even experienced ones — have to be reminded to be careful in the gym about grooming. Keep the following points in mind.

1. **Wear the right clothing.** Do not wear anything worn, loose or buckled which could get in the way of performance or interfere with the hands, feet or eyes.

2. **Do not wear jewellery.** Do not wear objects such as watches, bracelets, necklaces and so on. Glasses must be fastened securely.

3. **Check yourself.** Hair must never block the gymnast's vision. Tie it back if it is long. Also, make sure that the length of your nails does not interfere with your footing or grip.

4. **Keep your hands dry.** Gymnasts performing on the asymmetrical bars coat their hands in powder known as 'chalk' to keep their hands dry and therefore not slippery. This powder is, in fact, magnesium carbonate which absorbs sweat efficiently. Dry hands have a better grip on the bars then sweaty ones.

There are other safety rules more specifically concerned with training. Your club should have a copy of the *Gymnastics Safety Manual* published by The Pennsylvania State University Press from which these rules are taken:

5. Do not fool around near gymnastics equipment.
6. Before using apparatus, make sure it is properly adjusted and secured with sufficient mats around it.
7. Do not use apparatus without qualified supervision.
8. Use proper warm-up and conditioning exercises before trying new and forceful moves.
9. Learn new skills in the right order. Check with your coach.
10. Do not attempt a new skill without a qualified instructor at hand
11. Learn how to dismount properly from apparatus before doing so. Ask your coach.
12. Any movement where you could land on your back or neck is dangerous and could cause serious injury.
13. Any activity involving motion, rotation or height could also cause serious injury.
14. Do not train or perform if you feel ill.

Below: A coach shows a gymnast the mixed grip on the bars.

First aid

This element of danger in gymnastics means that every now and then, someone is injured in the gym. Every gym club should have a comprehensive first aid kit and every gymnast should know where it is. Every club should also have someone qualified in first aid. If you are injured in the gym, tell your coach, even if the injury seems a small one, as treatment on the spot may mean quick recovery. If you have more than a minor injury, do not start training again until you have fully recovered. Many gymnasts have found to their cost that they have aggravated injuries by not allowing them a longer time to heal. Serious injuries will mean that the victim will have to go to hospital immediately. But for injuries which do not need hospital care at once, it is worthwhile knowing what to do in case there is no one qualified in first aid present at the time.

1. If there is bleeding, clean the area thoroughly. Then stop the bleeding by direct pressure and apply a sterile dressing.
2. Otherwise apply ice or freezer spray. If the ice is in a plastic bag, remember to place some cotton material between the bag and the skin.
3. Put a firm application of crepe bandage or elastic strapping around the injury.
4. Raise the affected limb as high as possible for 20 to 30 minutes. Remember, again, speedy and correct first aid is very important in the treatment of minor gymnastics injuries.

Bruised hips. A tip for girls whose hips get bruised while training on the asymmetric bars is to use vinyl foam under the leotard for protection.

Your hands. You should take special care with your hands as they are subjected to hard punishment when you work on the asymmetric bars. Keep them clean, well-conditioned, and protected with handguards. This will help prevent acute soreness: Do not let callouses become large; they can be ripped off with painful results and take a long time to heal. So trim callouses down with a pumice stone or emery board. If you get blisters, let the skin become hard before you remove it. After you have done so, keep the area moist with Vaseline to prevent it cracking.

If your hands feel very sore, give them a rest from the asymmetric bars and concentrate on other training.

Finally, treat every moment in the gymnasium as an opportunity to learn something about the sport. Remember, you can learn from your fellow gymnasts, too. Mistakes, new ideas, new achievements — all will contribute to your knowledge of a sport in which you must use your brain as well as your body to gain the greatest satisfaction.

Opposite: Elena Naimushina (USSR) 'chalks up' the asymmetric bars with magnesium carbonate powder. This will reduce 'drag' on her hands when she performs her routine.

CHAPTER 3

THE VAULT

At one time, it was thought that only male gymnasts could excel at vaulting. Today, that view is proved wrong at every major international competition.

It is particularly important to master the art of vaulting well, since it is the opening piece in women's gymnastics competition. The better you vault, the more confidence you will gain for performing on the other apparatus.

In a women's gymnastics competition, the vault is the first piece in the order of the four apparatus events. It is also the piece which takes the shortest time to perform, consisting as it does of a run, the actual vault, (during which the gymnast must place her hands on the horse) and a landing. In voluntary exercises, however, women are allowed two attempts at the vault — scoring with the better of the two — and this extends the time taken by each performer on the piece.

Many gymnasts tend to treat the vault as a simple exercise because it is so brief. This is a mistaken attitude because the vault is exactly the same in terms of value when marked as the other pieces are. So obviously a gymnast should make sure that her vault for a competition is the very best that she can perform. First competitions for young gymnasts are usually based on vaulting and floorwork and this is another reason why the vault should not be neglected in training. This is not to say that this movement is unpopular with gymnasts; on the contrary, it appeals to performers of all standards because it involves the excitement of speed, flight and daring. Gymnasts who execute a good vault at the beginning of a competition will be elated not only by their favourable start (and therefore good marks) but also by a sense of satisfaction.

What is the origin of vaulting in gymnastics? Historians are agreed that the horse — the item of equipment over which gymnasts vault — began with the dummy wooden horse used by Roman soldiers many centuries ago. The wooden horses helped Roman cavalrymen to learn the technique of mounting and dismounting from real horses. Later, knights of the Middle Ages who rode into battle wearing armour also trained on wooden horses. Thus the wooden horse was regarded for a long time as training equipment to mount or jump on.

When gymnastics began to develop as a modern sport in the nineteenth century, the wooden horse was already in use. It was usually covered with leather and sported a neck, saddle, croup, and pommel handles for basic swinging and circling exercises, the first of which were devised by Ludwig Jahn. Soon vaulting or jumping over the horse became another development of gymnastics technique and before long, vaulting became a standard exercise for physical education in many countries, Britain included. The horse then changed in appearance to the familiar leather-top box.

Both men and women vault in gymnastics; men with the horse placed lengthways *(long horse)* and women with the horse placed sideways *(broad horse)*. For women, the horse must be adjusted to a height of 1m 20cm. The maximum width of the horse must be 1m 63cm. These measurements are laid down by the International

Gymnastics Federation (FIG). The run-up to the horse is made on a mat which is usually 24m in length. There are no rules about the actual length of run-up for women but leading coaches advise a minimum of 15m. An important item in vaulting is the springboard which helps the gymnast to gain elevation during the vault and can be used for mounting the asymmetric bars and beam as well. Specifications for the springboard are also drawn up by the FIG.

Below: The modern vaulting horse is the descendant of the dummy wooden horse on which Roman cavalrymen learned how to mount and dismount.

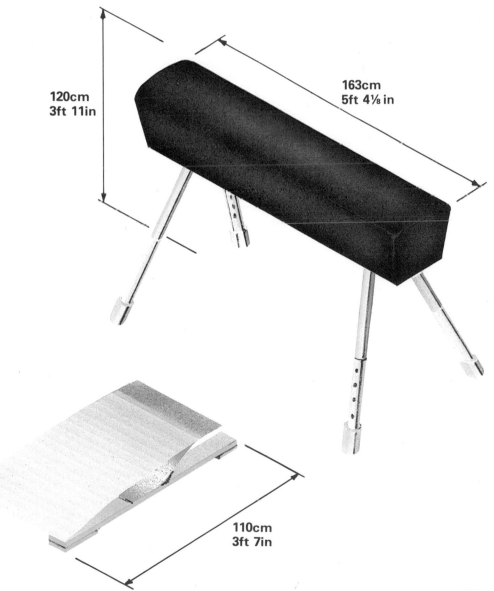

120cm
3ft 11in

163cm
5ft 4⅛ in

110cm
3ft 7in

Above: All vaults have six phases which follow each other in sequence. In them, except for the simplest vaults, the gymnast's body will turn on one of three axes, or a combination of more than one axis.

The rules governing competition vaulting and the three other gymnastics apparatus events are found in a book published by the FIG known as the *Code of Points.* As with the other apparatus pieces, vaulting is marked out of 10·00 points. Each vault has a rating which is found in the *Code of Points.* For example, a handspring vault will earn a gymnast a maximum of 9·40 points. Before her vault, if it is a voluntary one, the gymnast or her coach will indicate to the judges what vault she is going to perform. If her vault is very advanced and not in the *Code of Points,* a description of that vault has to be submitted to the authorities a month before the competition. In practice, however, only pioneering top gymnasts will perform advanced vaults other than the standard ones found in the *Code of Points.*

During the vault, points will be deducted for faults made by the gymnast. For example, bent legs can cost her up to 0·50 points as can insufficient height in her vault. The gymnast and her coach should be familiar with the general and specific faults which can lose her points. Interference by a coach once the gymnast has started her run can be penalized and could even make the vault void.

The marking for vaults in competitions is published in the *Code of Points.*

Analysis of a vault

When the human body turns, it rotates around an axis. Thus, in a cartwheel, the body turns on a front-back axis. In a spin, the rotation is around a vertical axis and in a somersault the body moves on a side axis.

In gymnastics, the simplest vaults feature no turns at all but as the gymnast progresses, she will learn vaults with a variety of turns in them. To sum up, vaults can be described as follows:

1. Straight vaults when the body does not turn at all.
2. Vaults around the side axis.
3. Vaults around the front-back axis.
4. Vaults around the vertical axis.
5. Vaults which combine turns around more than one body axis.

Whatever the vault, it will have six phases and each in its basic form must be understood by the gymnast. The phases are:

1. The run.
2. The take-off.
3. First flight.
4. Support position or thrust.
5. Second flight.
6. The landing.

Here is what the gymnast should aim to achieve during each phase:

The run. The gymnast must find a starting point for her run so that she reaches her maximum speed by the time of the take-off. She should measure her run so that she can start at the same distance from the horse wherever she competes. At the same time, she should count the number of paces in her run as this will help her timing on reaching the springboard. During the run itself, the gymnast will lean slightly forward with arms bent at the elbows, pumping backwards and forwards. She should run on her toes, increasing her speed.

In the last steps of the run, the gymnast will bring her arms quickly backwards before she jumps to land with both feet on the springboard prior to take-off. She must be careful not to slow her run at this point or make her last step too high. Before her feet touch the springboard, her arms must be swung forward quickly and upwards. Ideally, the upward motion of the arms will help depress the springboard thus giving the gymnast more power to her take-off.

The take-off. Legs and hips should be flexed slightly on the board with the body bent slightly at the hips. The more the body is bent at this stage, the more it will rotate, so for vaults which do not require considerable rotation the angle of lean should be slight. The push-up by the legs should not take place until the body's weight is ahead of the feet. The thrust of the legs should coincide with the upward stretch of the arms. So three forces must be used quickly to take the gymnast into first flight: the momentum of the run, the upwards stretch of the arms and the downward thrust of the legs.

Opposite: Two Natalias from the Soviet Union, Shaposhnikova and Yurchenko, prepare to begin their run-up to the horse.

The squat

First flight. This is the time between take-off and touching the horse. After take-off, the body will achieve maximum height with the feet moving to the rear. Factors affecting the movement of the feet in flight are the distance of the springboard from the horse and, as mentioned, how much the body is angled at take-off. For advanced vaults, the gymnast should develop a short, fast first flight. This will, of course, depend on the vault being attempted.

Support position. At this stage, the hands contact the horse parallel and flat with the fingers pointing in the direction of the vault. The hands must not be too wide apart. The shoulder joints should be flexed slightly and then stretched forcefully to give thrust upwards. This will maintain the body's lift.

Below: Speed, spring and thrust are the essentials of producing lift in a vault.

Straddle

Stoop

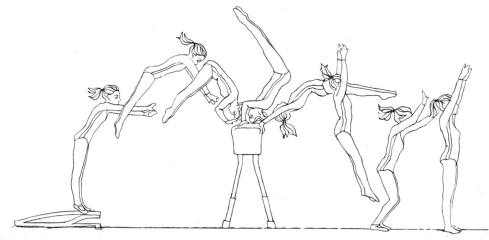

Headspring

Second flight. Each type of vault proceeds to the landing in a different way, with the body in varying positions or with actions such as twisting or somersaulting. Whatever vault the gymnast performs, she must end this phase with the body in a favourable position for a controlled landing.

The landing. In a perfect landing, the gymnast must stop on the ground without taking extra steps. Therefore she should arrive with her feet together and ahead of her body weight. Her knees should bend, but not too much, to absorb the horizontal pressure on her body to continue moving forwards. Her arms should be held up and back. Once landed, she should stand upright quickly.

Below: The landing is all-important for the gymnast. The more controlled it is, the better the impression made on judges and spectators.

Opposite: Elena Davydova executes a perfect landing.

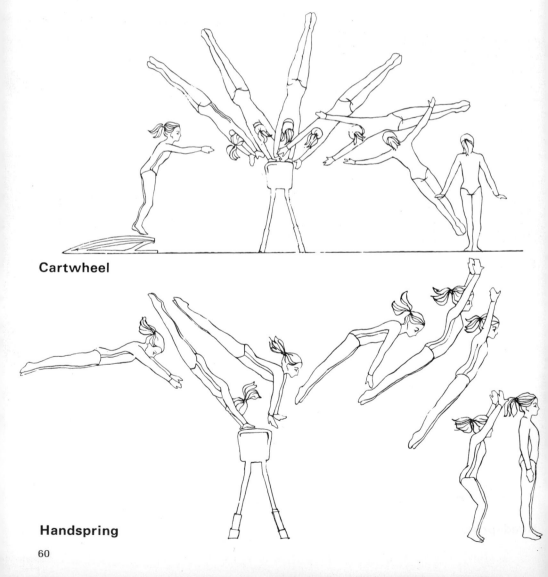

Cartwheel

Handspring

60

Safety

Gymnasts practising vaulting should be aware of the need to observe safety measures, particularly around the approach area and landing zone. Gymnasts working on other training should be careful not to obstruct vaulters and they must be ready to warn anyone who might cause an obstruction. No one should vault without adequate supervision and safety mats available.

Training

Before tackling new vaults, the gymnast must have practised the basic skills of vaulting and, indeed, sought to have improved her standards. Some gymnasts are apprehensive about learning the vault; after all, to throw one's body into the air at speed over an obstacle can be daunting. But training that is carefully planned can instil confidence in the most timid of girls. From the beginning, it should be realized that gymnasts need not train with the horse at its full height of 1m 20cm as for competitions. The useful box horse found in so many gyms is thus invaluable for young gymnasts who can then practise their skills with the box set at any convenient height.

Initial training for vaulting should concentrate on the six phases of the vault as described above. It should be remembered that as the phases follow each other in sequence, the success of each part depends to a large extent on how the preceding one was executed. So, taking each phase in turn with the fundamental ones first, here are some approaches which can help improve performances.

Yamashita

The run. The run must be fast and efficient, with even paces. This can be developed by sprinting over short distances between 20m and 50m. If the gymnast finds it hard to keep her paces even, she can mark her run with lines. To start the run, rise on the toes and overbalance forwards.

Take-off. The gymnast should practise the step on to the springboard so that it does not become a hurdle to her, physically and mentally. Basic training here can be jumping from a bench on to the springboard and then off. As the gymnast improves, she can jump on to the board from a short run which she can lengthen while increasing her speed. Remember that the feet must land ahead of the hips with the arms held well back. As the arms come forward and up, ankles and knees push down to create lift off the springboard. A box horse or stacked crash mats placed at a low height beyond the springboard will give the gymnast incentive to strive for greater lift.

Landing. Landing is the third major part of vaulting and its practice should be incorporated in basic training. The gymnast can practise the landing from a low height using the box horse longways on and then increase the height. The jump down must avoid excessive arching of the back and the body should be tense in the air.

Below: Training for vaulting is very much a matter of acquiring confidence.

First flight. The aim is to increase the distance of flight between the springboard and horse. One method of training is to jump off the springboard and dive on to stacked crash mats, finishing with a forward roll. To encourage the gymnast to gain height, a low box horse can be placed between the springboard and the crash mats. The height of the horse can then be raised as the gymnast gains confidence. The vaulting horse can be substituted for the crash mats once the gymnast has acquired lift and height in her first flight.

Support position. Exercises here must help to strengthen the shoulders and wrists. An effective way is to swing the legs up as for a handstand but not raising them

Below: There are several ways in which aids can be used to help gymnasts learn the six phases of a vault.

Hecht

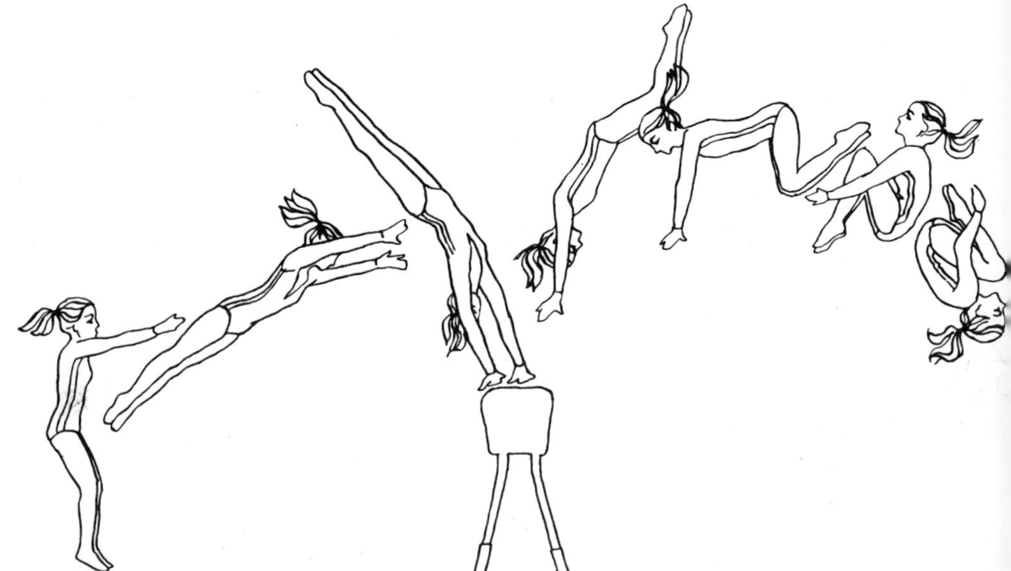

Tsukahara tucked

higher than 40°. Push strongly through the shoulders and either hop forward before placing the feet on the ground or push back on to the feet. A heavy weight such as a medicine ball can be held to the chest and thrust away as far as possible.

Second flight. Practice for the second flight, which ends in the landing, should ensure that the gymnast leaps high and covers as much distance as possible. As in training for the first flight, the gymnast can leap from the horse over a box horse with her body extended for the landing. A mark on the floor will give her a distance to aim for. Another exercise is to perform a handstand on the horse placed longways and then thrust with the arms, bringing the legs down to straddle the end of the horse before landing. This combines many elements of the vault but the gymnast will need support when trying it for the first time.

The vaults

As emphasized previously, the gymnast must master the simpler vaults before she attempts the more difficult ones. The group which follows is therefore of the basic kind and should be in every gymnast's 'repertoire'.

Basic vaults

The squat.
Straddle.
Stoop.
Headspring.
Squat with half turn.
Stoop with half turn.
Straddle with half turn.
Layout squat.
Layout straddle.
Layout stoop.
Cartwheel.
Handspring.

Now for vaults that call for more expertise. They should cause no great problem to the gymnast who learns her vaulting skills and movements thoroughly and progressively.

Advanced vaults

Cartwheel with quarter turn outward.
Hecht.
Yamashita.
Cartwheel with full turn outward.
Hecht with full turn.
Handspring with full turn.
Tsukahara tucked.
Tsukahara piked.
(Other advanced vaults may be taken from the *Code of Points*.)

Exercises to aid vaulting which can be undertaken at home.

These exercises, while particularly helpful to vaulters, can also form part of daily exercise routines.

1. Run on the spot with knees high, keeping on toes.
2. Skip with a rope.
3. Skip jump holding a weight to the chest.
4. Stand facing a wall and lean forward to support the body with one arm, the other held behind. Exchange arms, thrusting from the shoulder. Repeat rapidly.
5. Lie on your stomach with the thumbs linked behind the back. Bend the trunk backwards, so that the chest comes off the floor. Relax and repeat.

Gymnasts should set themselves a time limit for each exercise, say fifteen seconds, so that the performance of the exercise is balanced.

Finally, the keen gymnast will study the vaulting of other gymnasts so that she can recognise both faults and good points and relate them to her own experience. She should correct any defects in style that she might have at an early stage; otherwise they will be hard to change later on.

Opposite: Careful training on the vault is inevitably rewarded with good marks in competition.

Below: Keys to good elevation in vaulting are velocity from the run-up and thrust from arms and legs.

CHAPTER 4

THE FLOOR

The floor exercise is the
highspot of a competition
for the gymnast, and titles
are won or lost at this
stage.

The floor exercise in a women's gymnastics competition is the last one to be performed. It is usually welcomed with excitement for several reasons, and not only because it can be the climax to a closely-fought competition. In the first place, the floor exercise is a demonstration of natural movements. No equipment, apart from the mat on which the exercise is performed, is used to restrict the freedom of the gymnast. The basic movements of the floor exercise — and there are several — influence movements on the other apparatus. For example, the handstand and the somersault which gymnasts first learn on the floor, can be elements of moves performed on asymmetric bars, beam and vault.

Thus floorwork is the root of gymnastics and every gymnast learns skills on the floor as a first step. But the floor exercise is more than a collection of movements — it is a medium for the gymnast to express herself artistically. The big factor here is that the floor exercise is performed to music which links it firmly to art in the shape of dance. For just over a minute, the gymnast can project her personality through this combination of acrobatic skills and artistic expression to reach the imagination of her audience.

Show business? Perhaps in part, but floorwork is easily the most popular piece with audiences, and an exercise creatively performed will earn the gymnast her best applause of the competition.

Strangely enough, the floor exercise as we know it today is fairly new in gymnastics. It has its origins in the massed exercises staged in the nineteenth century in which hundreds of performers took part. There are still massed events at gymnastics festivals held in Europe, but these have very little connection with the modern floor exercise. As will be realized, massed displays have to be performed in large spaces, often outdoors, and when the modern Olympic Games were established in 1896, this pattern of gymnastic exercises was maintained. However, economy demanded in later Olympics that the number of performers, who were mostly men, were reduced. This in turn meant that the floor exercise lost the rigid formality which had previously been so necessary. By 1932 at the Los Angeles Olympic Games, men were performing an individual floor exercise for the first time. There are still massed events held at gymnastics festivals in Europe but these have no connection with the modern floor exercise.

For women, the individual floor exercise was included in a world competition for the first time at the World Championships of 1950. Six years later at the Melbourne Olympic Games, one of the greatest performers ever on the floor, Larissa Latynina of the Soviet Union won her first world gold medal on the piece. She was to win three other world medals for the floor exercise before she retired from international competition in 1965.

The modern floor exercise is performed on a square area 12m × 12m. For major competitions, the area consists of panels of elastically joined plywood layers on a rubber base. These layers are bonded by inserts with shock absorbent foam and covered with nylon carpet. The area is designed to absorb the shocks of the tumbling skills of the gymnasts, and is the only piece of equipment in gymnastics with exactly the same specifications for men and women.

Below: The whole of the floor area should be used during a floor exercise routine.

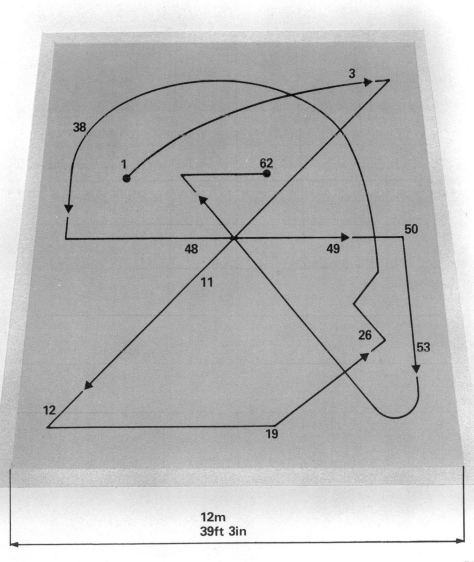

12m
39ft 3in

The women's floor exercise, then, is a combination of acrobatics, tumbling and dance. It should include leaps, turns, balances and poses. The gymnast must utilize the entire 12m square (but without going outside it) for no less than 1 minute and not more than 1·30 minutes. As the *Code of Points* states: 'The clock will be started when the gymnast begins her exercise with a movement. It will stop when the gymnast remains in a stationary final pose. A signal will warn the gymnast at 1·25 minutes and a second time at 1·30 minutes. If the gymnast ends the exercise at the second signal, the exercise is considered to have corresponded to regulations.

The gymnast must link all movements together in a harmonious way that suits her personality and her build. The movements themselves should be balanced throughout the routine, and the whole must flow to a rhythm — and variations of it — according to the character of the music.

When planning her routine, the gymnast must pay heed to the requirements of the *Code of Points*. The routine must contain at least seven 'difficulties' which are movements found in the *Code*. These difficulties are either 'medium' or 'superior' and in a floor routine three of the seven must be of superior rating. The routine must also include at least two groups of acrobatic movements and the final part should contain either a move or acrobatic combination of superior difficulty.

Opposite and below:
Suzanne Dando is one of Britain's leading gymnasts. In 1979, she became British Champion for the floor exercise.

How is the floor exercise marked? It is marked out of 10, in the same way as the asymmetric bars and beam are. Judges deduct points according to the faults committed by the gymnast.

In voluntary exercises, the points are distributed as follows:

Difficulty 3·00. For each missing 'superior difficulty', the gymnast is penalized 0·6 points and for each 'medium difficulty' not included she will have 0·3 deducted.

Originality and value of connections 0·5. The judges consider how well the movements are linked and deduct accordingly.

Composition 0·5. If the routine has been well-planned and balanced in its elements, the gymnast will earn maximum points.

Execution and amplitude 4·00. In this section, the gymnast is judged on the way she performs the exercise. Posture, balance, steadiness and flexibility all count here. Amplitude means performing each movement in the fullest possible way.

General impression 1·0. If the gymnast makes a good impression on the judges, she will not lose out here.

In compulsory exercises, the gymnast has to perform according to the routine prepared for an actual competition. These exercises are also marked out of 10, with deductions as before for not including medium or

Below: The gymnast must understand what elements are required for her routine and how it is judged.

Handstand

Forward roll

74

superior difficulties and penalties of up to 0·2 for making small changes to the exercise.

General deductions. The gymnast can lose points for faults outside the classification of her performance. This list from the *Code of Points* gives some examples to keep in mind.

1. Fall on the floor: 0·5.
2. Support with one or two hands: 0·50.
3. Cross the boundary line with one or two feet or other parts of the body: each time 0·10.
4. Absence of acrobatic series: each time 0·20.
5. Repetition of a missed element: 0·50.
6. Fall in rhythm of the exercise *as a whole*: 0·50.
in part: each time 0·20.
7. Musical accompaniment against regulations: 1·00.
8. Exercise does not end with music: 0·30.
9. Exercise without music: 1·00.
10. Missing beginning of exercise through personal error: 0·50.
11. Assistance by the pianist (if a pianist is used): each time 0·20.
12. Exercise too long: 0·30.
13. Exercise too short: for each missing section 0·05.
14. Coach is present on the podium: 0·50.
15. Coach signals gymnast: 0·30.
16. Start of the exercise without music: 0·20.

Below: As well as knowing how a floor exercise is judged, the gymnast must be aware of other ways she can forfeit points.

Handstand forward roll

Backward roll

Music. Ideally, the gymnast should have the services of a pianist available to accompany her during her floor exercise. A pianist can adapt, even compose a piece of music which can be tailored to fit the routine as well as reflect the personality of the gymnast. But for most gymnasts, music for the floor exercise means taped music. Whatever music is chosen, it must suit the movements or else the gymnast will lose points. The music must be played on one instrument which may not be the electric piano, accordian or organ. In practice, this means the piano. So the gymnast must look out for music which appeals to her and which has variations of mood or rhythm around which a routine can be created. The music may have a brief introduction to give the gymnast a cue for starting her routine.

Check list

The following list will help the gymnast to construct the floor exercise routine which she can perform to her best ability.

1. The routine should emphasize the gymnast's strong points and play down skills which are poorly performed. For example, if the gymnast is particularly flexible in performing the splits, her routine should show this. Or, if she is very still in some limbs, the routine should avoid movements which emphasize this. Weak points must, however, be worked on for improvement during training.
2. Choose medium and superior difficulties which the gymnast can learn and use well. Select as many difficult actions as possible.
3. Find styles and moods of expression which suit the gymnast's personality. For example, an extrovert girl would need a livelier approach than a serious girl.
4. Make up some new movements for the routine. These could be steps or linkages, variations or combinations of movements.
5. Watch that the same element or position is not repeated exactly. An element can be repeated up to three times (with the exception of the back flip) if it is for an eye-catching purpose or to reflect a type of move. If an element is varied, started or finished differently, it is not considered a repetition.
6. Vary: speed and rhythm (which must match the music); body level; direction; distribution and combination of elements (which must link together smoothly); type of movement and body position (including arm and leg positions).
7. Use movements which you enjoy performing
8. Be aware of the general impression: posture, expression, presentation and so on.

Flexibility

When the gymnast has conscientiously and regularly carried out her suppling exercises as shown already on page 43, she will find her body becoming more and more flexible and ready to learn movements for the floor exercise and the other apparatus. Here are two more suppling exercises — to help side splits development and ankle suppleness. Remember that the body must be warmed up before undertaking any exercise that demands stretching of muscles.

1. Lie on the floor and place the seat and legs against a wall, legs pointing up. Open the legs and slide them down the wall as far as possible. Hold the legs in this position for a few minutes.

2. Kneel with the tips of the feet on the floor. Lean backwards so that the knees lift from the floor slightly. Again, hold this position for as long as possible.

Below: Once a gymnast is supple, she can tackle a variety of moves in the floor exercise.

Split position

Double bent-leg position

Yogi hand stand

Movements

These movements and positions will give the gymnast an excellent foundation from which to create her routines. The examples are given in the order of difficulty and the gymnast should try and master each one before going on to the next. Because these movements are essentially gymnastic and acrobatic, the gymnast must search for ways to express them as with dance movements, as part of a comprehensive floor routine.

Floor movements

Forward roll.
Backward roll.
Handstand.
Handstand forward roll.
Headspring.
Dive forward roll.
Forward walkover.
Cartwheel.
Round-off.
Backward roll to handstand.
Front handspring.

Below: Movements in a floor routine are performed in sequence, so the gymnast must devise natural links between them.

Forward walkover

Cartwheel

Tinsica.
Back flip.
Back walkover.
Valdez.
Front somersault.
Back somersault.
Aerial cartwheel.

Leaps
Split leap.
Stag leap.
Arch jump.

Stands
Arabesque.
Arched stand.
Scale backward.

Body waves
Body wave forward.
Body wave backward.
Body swing forward upward — to stage jump.
(Other movements and positions may be taken from the
Code of Points.)

Below: The experienced
gymnast will always try
to improve her floor
routine — especially when
she is competing
regularly.

Round-off

Backward roll to handstand

Front handspring

Back flip

Above: The Soviet Union was the first country to link gymnastics training with that of ballet. This development has been followed by every leading gymnastics country.

Opposite: Ruth Adderley of the Ladywell Gymnastics Club was a British international in the early 1970s. Here she is in the middle of her floor exercise.

Ballet exercises

Because dance movements form such an important part of the floor exercise, leading gymnastics coaches are making sure that their gymnasts receive some form of ballet training. Ballet exercises are valuable in two ways. They help the gymnast to improve the elegance and poise of her body and they add strength to the back and legs. Ballet has three fundamental leg movements which contract and relax the muscles and which the gymnast can perform in the gymnasium or at home. They are: the *plié* (bending of the knees), the *relève* (rising to the ball of the foot) and the *battement tendu* (when the foot is stretched from a closed position to a pointed position on the floor). There are three positions of the feet from which to perform these exercises.

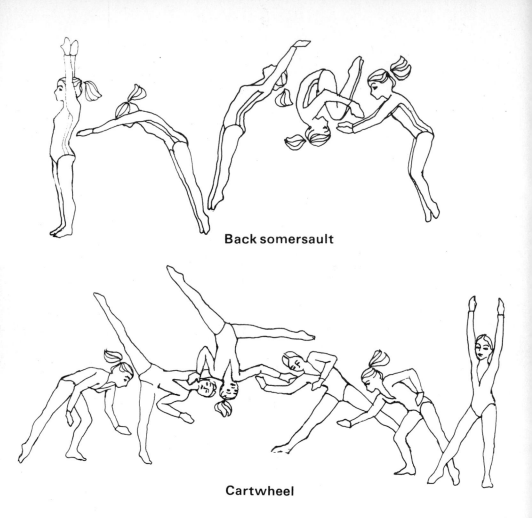

Back somersault

Cartwheel

Above: All ballet dancers train at the *barre,* a long railing, and gymnasts can use gymnasium equipment for the same purpose.

The gymnast should perform the following exercises holding a *barre*. This is the name given to the long railing at which ballet dancers train, but gymnasts can use the balance beam or the backs of chairs.

1. Face the *barre*, holding it lightly with both hands and with feet in first position. *Demi-plié* (bend knees, keeping heels on floor, straighten). *Relève* (rise to toes, lower heels). *Grand plié* (lower body until thighs are almost parallel to the floor and keeping body straight). *Relève* and repeat.

2. Repeat in second position. The heels should remain on the floor throughout *grand plié* in this position.

3. Repeat the first exercise but stand sideways to the *barre* holding with one hand and raising the other arm sideways to just below shoulder height in a gentle curve.

4. Repeat the second exercise standing sideways.

5. For the *battement tendu*, stand sideways to the *barre* with feet in the third position holding with one hand. Slide the outside foot forward along the floor until the heel has to be raised. Then arch the foot through the ball of the foot until the toes are pointed but still in contact with the floor. The leg must be turned out from the hip. Return the foot to the starting position and repeat to the side. Then repeat to the rear. On returning the foot, face the other way and repeat with the other foot. Careful performance of the *battement tendu* can strengthen the feet considerably.

The successful floor exercise has to be planned and practised again and again, but once the gymnast has found the routine which suits her and which stands out from those of her competitors, there is no greater thrill than performing to an appreciative audience.

Above: Ballet exercises can be performed in a class to music under the direction of a teacher or coach. Some clubs use the services of a dance teacher for ballet training.

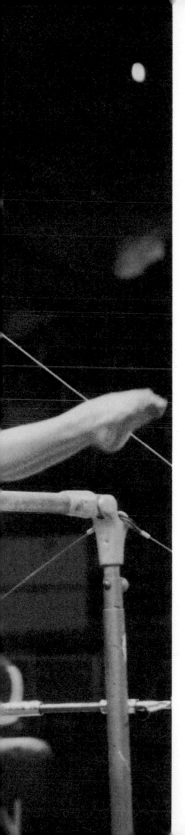

CHAPTER 5

THE ASYMMETRIC BARS

The asymmetric bars is an exciting, punishing apparatus requiring strength and concentration, and including an element of danger. Do not, however, be daunted by the asymmetric bars – simply treat them with respect.

Asymmetric bars, high-and-low bars, uneven parallel bars — there are several names for this exciting piece of apparatus in women's gymnastics. But whatever gymnasts call the bars, they are all agreed on one fact: the asymmetric bars is the hardest piece of the four apparatus to learn. Why should this be?

The bars require strength, speed, suppleness, balance and timing; qualities which cannot be developed without considerable training. The asymmetric bars, too, is a punishing exercise, causing bruised thighs where the gymnast hits the equipment at speed and calloused hands from swinging on the bars. The difficulty of the piece is further complicated in that the bars present the gymnast with a very wide range of skills to master. This also means that leading international gymnasts are continually producing new and thrilling movements on the bars.

The asymmetric bars are a variation of the parallel bars used by male gymnasts and which were developed in the nineteenth century by Ludwig Jahn, the father of gymnastics. Jahn only evolved the parallel bars because he needed a piece of equipment to help young German men improve their work on the pommelled horse. The parallel bars were thus designed to enable gymnasts to gain arm and shoulder strength.

Until the 1930s, women used the parallel bars for exercise but it became clear that the piece demanded such strength that it was unsuitable for women. As a result, modifications were made to the parallel bars so that one bar was almost a metre below the other. This new equipment was demonstrated at the 1936 Olympic Games in Berlin and was used for the first time in the Games at Helsinki in 1952. Since then, the skills on the asymmetric bars have developed along the lines of those performed on the men's horizontal bar and consist mostly of swinging and circling movements.

The modern apparatus, then, consists of two bars, each 3·5m long. The high bar is set at 2·3m from the ground and the low bar, which is flush with the high bar, is at a height of 1·5m. The gymnast may widen or narrow the horizontal distance between the bars to suit her height and reach by means of two handles. The maximum distance the bars may be apart is ·78m and the minimum ·43m. Each bar must be 4·2cm in width and 4·8cm in height. As mentioned previously, for certain movements when the gymnast mounts the bars, she can leap from a springboard which is used for vaulting. In competition, the asymmetric bars is the second piece of apparatus, following the vault.

Apart from swinging movements, which dominate, an asymmetric bars' routine must include bar changes (the gymnast has to move to, and perform on, each bar frequently), changes of support positions on the bars,

Opposite: The specification for the asymmetric bars is published in the *Code of Points.* The gymnast can alter the distance between the bars to suit her height and reach.

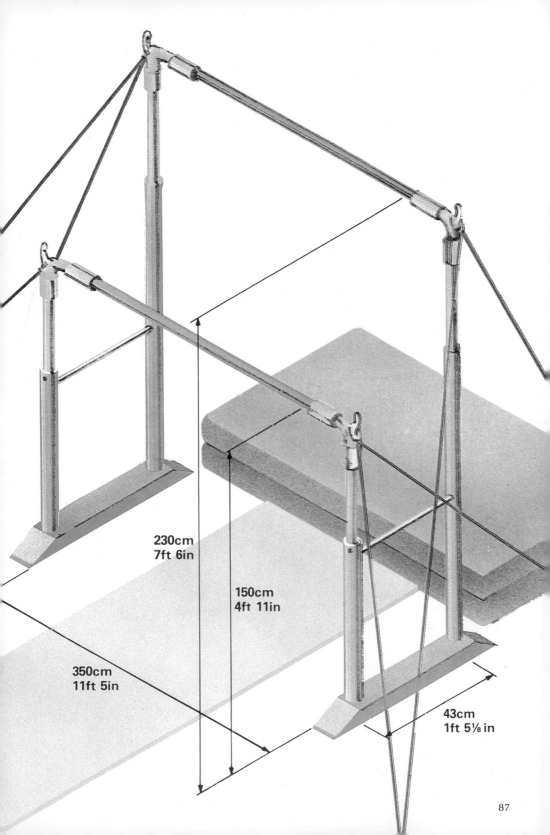

230cm
7ft 6in

150cm
4ft 11in

350cm
11ft 5in

43cm
1ft 5⅛ in

and changes in direction of movement, all without stops or pauses. The gymnast may dismount (land) only from swinging movements and not from a stationary position. She is allowed thirty seconds to remount the bars. If she fails to do so, her routine is judged to be completed. She is also allowed a run for her mount but must not run under the bars or touch them. As with the floor and beam exercises, a bars routine must include at least seven difficulties from the *Code of Points* — three superior and four medium. The gymnast is marked in the same way as in the floor exercise.

General deductions. Points may be deducted from the gymnast's score on the asymmetric bars if she or her coach commit the following faults:

1. Fall on the floor or apparatus: 0·50 points.
2. Release one hand without additional support: 0·30 points.
3. Release one hand with additional support (foot on bar, against the apparatus or on the floor): 0·50 points.
4. Touching the bar or the floor: up to 0·50 points.
5. Intermediate swing (swing from knees): 0·50 points.
6. Repetition or a missed element: 0·50 points.

Below: Olga Korbut was an accomplished performer on the asymmetric bars. She won silver medals for this apparatus at the 1972 Olympic Games and the 1974 World Championships.

7. Dismount from a stationary position: 0·40 points.
8. Insufficient composition: up to 0·50 points.
9. Stop in the exercise: 0·20 points each time.
10. Running under the apparatus or touching bars before mount: 0·50 points.
11. Running under the apparatus after completion of the exercise: 0·30 points.
12. Coach stands between bars or runs under apparatus: 0·50 points.
13. Assistance during exercise (coach touches gymnast): 1·0 points.
14. Assistance during dismount: 0·50 points.

Below: Most gymnasts check the asymmetric bars before their routine for adjustment.

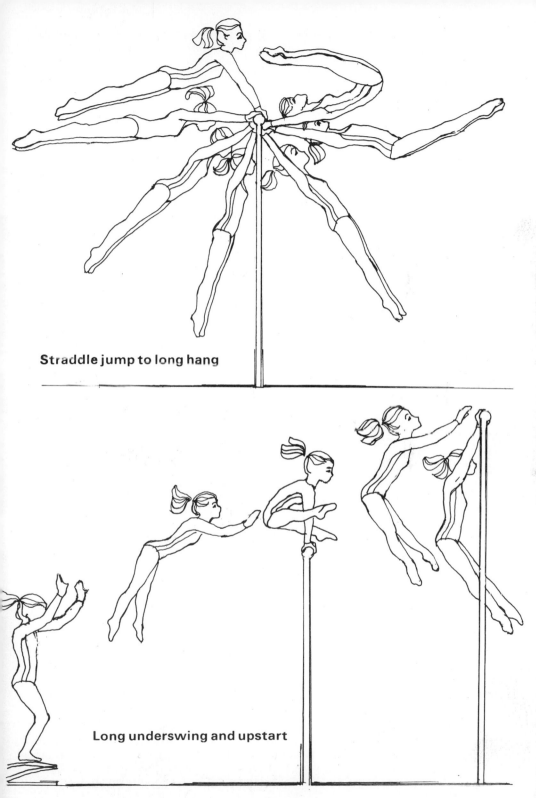

Straddle jump to long hang

Long underswing and upstart

Above: A gymnast's hands are most important to her for bar work. She must make sure that they are cared for; otherwise the asymmetric bars could be damaging and painful to them.

Training

In training for the asymmetric bars, the gymnast must take care of her hands. As indicated before, she must use hand lotion to help protect the skin of her palms, she must wear handguards from the start, and she should 'chalk' her hands before she works on the bars.

Her body preparation must aim to improve the strength of her arms, shoulders and stomach area and she should carry out exercises for this purpose. Some examples have been given on page 44 and more are shown at the end of this section. The gymnast should also aim to become supple in the hips.

Many asymmetric bars skills can be learned on a single bar and, if it will give the gymnast more confidence during early stages, the bar can be set lower than the official height. Plenty of mats should be used around

the bars to cushion falls, and a coach or qualified teacher should supervise all training.

We have seen how the box horse and stacked crash mats set at different heights can be useful in training for the vault. In the same way, these items of equipment can be very helpful when the gymnast is tentatively practising moves for the first time. An unconventional aid used with great success by former British national coach Pauline Prestidge is the humble broom handle held horizontally to recreate the position of the lower bar. This can help the gymnast become familiar with certain positions. Some gym clubs, especially new ones, may not have the use of a full set of asymmetric bars, but this should not stop their gymnasts from preparing themselves for work on the bars.

There are four grips on the bars with which the

Above: To guard against bruising while training, the bars can be padded with foam.

Opposite: This gymnast is demonstrating front support on the high bar. Front support is a basic position in bar work and is used on the beam as well.

gymnast must familiarize herself. The three most commonly used ones are regular grip, reverse grip and mixed grip. The fourth, used more as a 'catch' than a grip is dislocation.

The gymnast must use the right grip for the movement she is performing. The basic support positions on the bar all employ the regular grip. The positions are: front support, back support, mill support, long hang and piked hang.

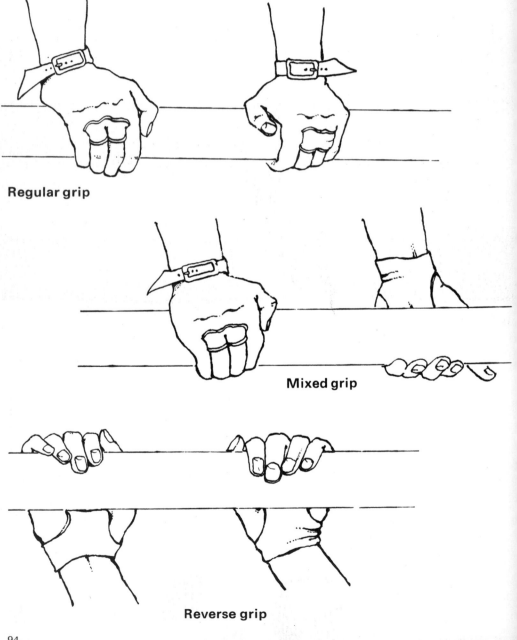

Regular grip

Mixed grip

Reverse grip

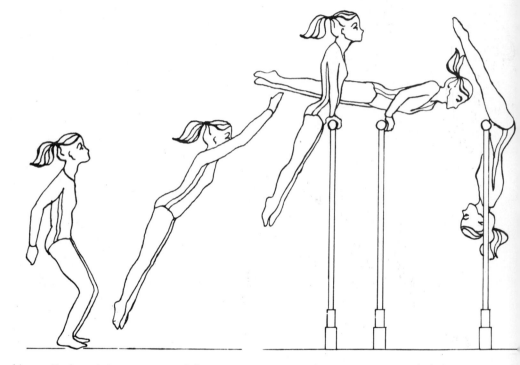

Above: Early training on the asymmetric bars should include swinging practice. This will help the gymnast to strengthen her grip and give her confidence.

A basic movement on the asymmetric bars is swinging, and the gymnast should spend some time getting used to swinging backwards and forwards in long hang on the practice bar. Swinging practice helps to develop grip strength as well as self confidence. The hands should be in regular grip and the arms straight, and the gymnast must keep her body straight as she swings. She must also aim to swing her body up to an almost horizontal position. At the end of the backward swings, she should try and release her hands and grasp the bar again before swinging forward once more.

When she can swing smoothly and easily, the gymnast should try making half-turns when her body is approaching the horizontal. This is performed by

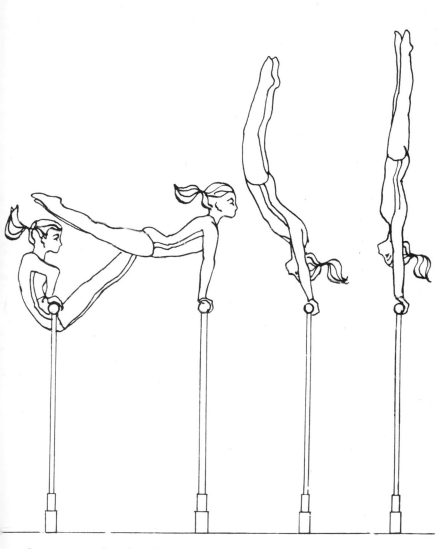

releasing one hand and turning towards the hand still grasping the bar. After this half-turn, the bar is grasped again, with the hands in mixed grip. At the end of the rear swing, the hands can let go to grasp in regular grip again. Half turns can be made at the end of alternate swings but remember that releasing each hand in turn will cause the gymnast to 'travel' along the bar.

An important 'swing' is the underswing which forms part of many movements on the bars. This is achieved by the gymnast holding the bar at arm's length in regular grip and jumping back and up, thus gaining height before swinging forwards, to stretch the legs straight out in front. In fact, the whole body should be extended at the end of the swing forward.

Above: Swinging practice should include half-turns and underswings as these can be used in routines.

From swinging, the gymnast progresses to circling the bar. Hip circles, for example, can be performed forward or backward from front support. In the backward hip circle, the gymnast swings her legs first forward then back so that she is horizontal, with her shoulders over the bar and her arms straight. On the return forward swing, her hips come to the bar and her shoulders drop back for the circle round the bar to return to front support. In the forward hip circle, the gymnast falls forward with her body slightly piked or bent forward from the waist. Her hands should move under the bar ahead of the gymnast to be ready to help swing back to front support. The bar must be kept close to the hips.

Another circle to practise is the mill circle from mill support, which may also be performed forwards or backwards. In forward hip and mill circles, the gymnast can reach out to catch the high bar if the movement is being performed on the low one. This can be done when the gymnast is facing outwards (away from the high bar)

Long hang on high bar, kip up to front support

and when she is approaching the upright position again.

Further circles to master are the seat circles — forward and backward — and sole circles. The seat circles are commenced in the back support position. For the back seat circle, the gymnast lifts her legs to the piked position, hands in regular grip. She then drops back and circles the bar to return to the back support position. In the front seat circle, the gymnast's hands must be in reverse grip. She falls forward to a piked position from which she unfolds as she swings around to the back support position again.

Sole circles on the low bar lead on to other movements such as catching the high bar or dismounting. They are performed in the straddle or stoop position with the feet on the bar, and the gymnast can circle forward or backward. As with other movements on the asymmetric bars, sole circles must be regarded as elements of one smooth continuous routine.

The gymnast must be accustomed to straddle or squat

Dislocation catch

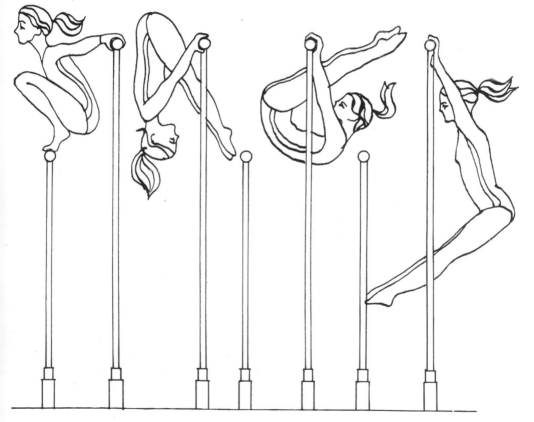

Above: The gymnast should only learn new positions or movements with the help of a qualified coach or teacher.

on the bars as these, too, are basic parts of other movements. The handstand, an element used on all four pieces of apparatus, should be practised as well. To repeat: new positions or movements must be learned with the aid and support of a qualified coach or teacher.

Once basic skills have been practised and learned

Underswing dismount

comprehensively, the gymnast can increase her repertoire by tackling more advanced moves. These can be placed into the following groups: mounts, upward swings and circles, kips (A kip is when the body is raised from a hang position to a support one), handstands, pirouettes, somersaults and dismounts.

Above: When the gymnast has acquire confidence by lear basic skills, she ca to practise more advanced move

The following are examples of well-known advanced moves which can be seen in top competitions.

Mounts

Long underswing and upstart.

Straddle jump to long hang.

Free jump to front support on high bar.

Free jump with ½ turn to long hang.

Free jump with ½ turn to front support on high bar.

Jump to front support, hip circle to handstand.

Upward swings and circles

Free jump to front support on high bar.

Upstart from low bar to high bar.

Long swing and backward hip circle.

Dislocation catch.

Rear support to rear support on high bar.

Rear lying hang, stoop through, kip to rear support.

Kips

Long hang on high bar, kip up to front support.

Below: A routine on the asymmetric bars has to be planned so that the movements flow naturally after each other.

Hecht dismount

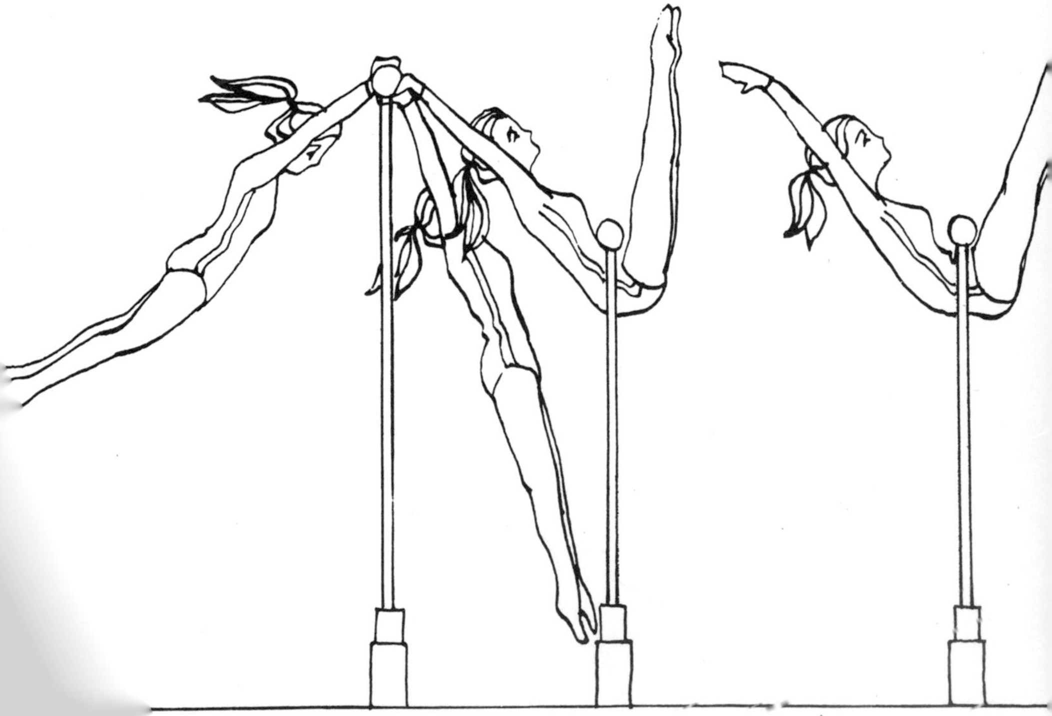

Outer rear support, ¾ seat circle.

Glide kip with ½ turn to rear support on low bar. A pirouette movement.

Handstands

Handstand from low bar to high bar.

Front support, hip circle to handstand.

Somersaults

Korbut.

Radochla.

Squat stand on low bar to back somersault tucked to catch high bar.

Janz roll.

Dismounts

Underswing dismount.

Handstand dismount.

Hecht dismount.

Jump to handstand, straddle or stoop off.

Stoop on high bar, forward somersault off.

Above: The handstand, which is a basic floor skill, can be incorporated into routines on the asymmetric bars.

Opposite: From front support, the gymnast can circle the bar to front support again.

To sum up, the asymmetric bars require many skills from the gymnast and these must be learned progressively. Only by learning them carefully, can the gymnast hope to become a competent performer on this difficult apparatus. The asymmetric bars also demand bravery in the execution of certain spectacular moves and this is another good reason to tackle the bars at a sure and steady pace. Once the bars are mastered, however, the gymnast will enjoy the challenge of risk, speed and timing.

CHAPTER 6

THE
BALANCE
BEAM

To the uninitiated,
performing on the beam
looks simple. In reality,
however, it requires superb
balance and concentration.
Once a young gymnast has
mastered the basic skills
involved in a beam routine,
she will have made great
progress towards becoming
a first-class gymnast.

To the spectator, a performance on the balance beam seems the most leisurely of all gymnastics exercises. The gymnast gives the impression of taking her time; nowhere in her routine is there a place for speed as there is on the other three apparatus. No wonder the beam is beloved of photographers, because this serenity which is so much a feature of beam work can be captured by the camera without much difficulty. However, the role of the beam has changed in recent times so that it is now much more than a means for women to demonstrate simple balances. It is true to say that almost any tumbling skill which is performed on the floor can be executed by top gymnasts on the beam.

The Swedish pioneer Pehr Henrik Ling used a version of the beam in the mid-nineteenth century. Apart from

Below: In recent years, a major improvement was made to the beam by the addition of a chamois leather-type covering which makes the surface less slippery and therefore safer for the gymnast.

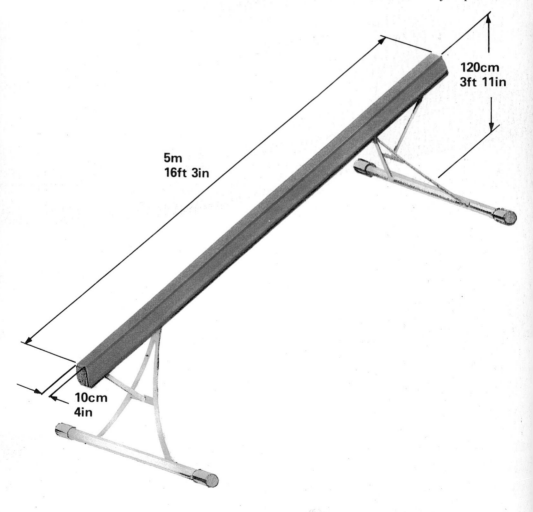

120cm
3ft 11in

5m
16ft 3in

10cm
4in

developing a sense of balance, the beam was used to encourage good posture, co-ordination and grace. The apparatus was unique in that it was designed exclusively with women in mind. There is no equivalent of the beam in men's gymnastics. The greatest advance in beam technique has been, as could be expected, during the last twenty-five years. The world's top gymnasts today show what a versatile piece the beam is by the range of movement which can be performed on it.

But balance is still the key to successful performing on the beam. The gymnast has to perform on a long, narrow platform which is 5m long and only 10cm wide. What is more, the beam is 1·2m high off the ground and thus the young gymnast can be forgiven if at first she finds the idea of performing on the beam daunting.

Below: Svetlana Agapova of the Soviet Union is about to perform a Valdez move on the beam. This means that she will move backwards to a handstand position.

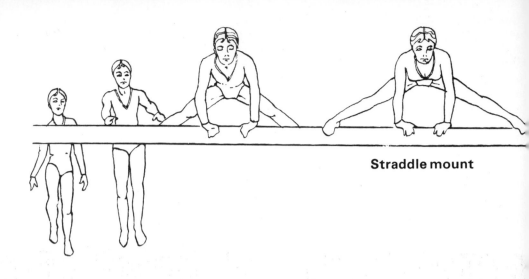

Straddle mount

Above: When a gymnast and her coach compose a beam routine, they must follow the regulations laid down in the *Code of Points.*

Let us see what the beam exercise requires of the gymnast.

Composition. The beam exercise is essentially one of balance composed of acrobatic and gymnastics movements. According to the *Code of Points*, the exercise should contain elements of balance, turns and pivots (one being a 360° turn moving forward, backward or sideways), leaps, jumps and hops (one of these must be a large one), steps and running combinations, acrobatic parts and connections, and elements close to the beam and above the beam.

The gymnast's routine must also keep to these rules:

1. There must be harmonious and dynamic change between the groups of movements.
2. The gymnast must avoid any repetition of movements but if she does repeat an element, she must perform it with a different connection or linkage.
3. Difficulties must be spread throughout the entire exercise.
4. The gymnast must use the whole length of the beam.
5. The mount and dismount must be in harmony to the difficulty of the exercise.
6. The gymnast should try not to use too many sitting and lying positions.

Rhythm. While the rhythm of the exercise must vary from lively to slow it must always flow smoothly without interruption. The gymnast should be careful not to perform an exercise that is not only slow and monotonous but also punctuated with pauses. Three stops are, however, permitted during the exercise:

Squat on mount

1. After planned, technically good and consciously held positions.
2. After any acrobatic stand such as the headstand or shoulder stand.
3. After gymnastic stands with held positions at the end of the movement.

Pauses before and after acrobatic elements can be penalized by 0·20 points each.

Duration. The time limit of the beam exercise is between 1·15 min and 1·35 min. Timekeeping starts when the gymnast's feet have left the floor or springboard and finishes when they touch the floor again as she finishes the routine. A signal warns the gymnast when she reaches 1·30 min and again when she comes up to 1·35. If she has dismounted at the second signal, her dismount and the duration of the exercise will be regarded as corresponding to the rules. The *Code of Points* further states that all elements executed after 1·35 minutes will not be evaluated. If the required difficulties have not been executed during the 1·35 minutes, an additional deduction of 0·30 points or 0·60 points will be made, depending on the value of the difficulty.

Falls. Rarely does a competition pass without a gymnast falling from the beam. If a gymnast falls, she will be penalized as indicated below. She may, however, continue the exercise, if she remounts within 10 seconds. If she fails to remount after the 10 seconds are up, the exercise is considered to have ended.

Approach. The gymnast is allowed one additional approach run if she has not touched the beam on her first.

Above: Outside her actual performance on the beam, the gymnast can be penalized for such faults as exceeding the time limit laid down or falling from the beam. She must therefore be familiar with how points can be deducted from her score whether they are connected with her movements or not.

Deductions. As with the other apparatus, the competitive gymnast must be aware of the penalties she may incur during a beam routine.

1. Fall on the floor or on the beam: 0·50 points.
2. Support with the hands on the beam to maintain balance: 0·50 points.
3. Touching beam after run (without mounting): 0·50 points.
4. Touching beam with hands to maintain balance: 0·30 points.
5. Support of a leg against the side of the beam: 0·20 points.
6. Additional movements of the body to maintain balance: 0·30 points.
7. Additional arm or leg movements to maintain balance: 0·20 points.

Below: Familiarity with and confidence in working on the narrow platform of the beam must be the gymnast's first aim.

8. More than three unmotivated stops: each time 0·20 points.
9. Poor head position during entire exercise: 0·20 points.
10. One full turn (360°) or large leap missing: each 0·20 points.
11. Exercise too long (after 1·35 min), exercise considered finished: 0·30 points.
12. Exercise too short (less than 1·15 min): for each missing second 0·05 points.
13. Coach present on podium during exercise: 0·50 points.
14. Coach signals gymnast: 0·30 points.
15. Monotony of rhythm in part: 0·20 points.
16. Monotony during the exercise: 0·50 points.

All these rules and deductions are laid down in the *Code of Points* by the FIG.

Below: Gesture, expression, movement— these must harmonize as naturally and smoothly as possible.

inental Sports

Training

In body preparation for beam work, the gymnast must aim to acquire suppleness, strength and spring. These qualities are, of course, among those she needs for the other apparatus. But now the gymnast also needs balance.

It has been noted that it takes courage for the young gymnast to perform on a narrow platform chest-high above the ground. Therefore the first skill that the gymnast should acquire in beam activity is that of becoming used to moving on the beam. This means spending a great deal of time first of all walking, then running, and then turning and jumping on the beam. But no-one expects the gymnast to begin her beam training on the high beam. In ideal conditions she will have the use of a low beam. If there is no low beam available, a bench such as those used in schools can be used, particularly for skills involving rolls, cartwheels and handstands.

One very important point about training for the beam is to remember that all skills should be first learned at floor level. Then and only then should the gymnast perform them on the low beam before moving to a higher beam. The gymnast's coach will make sure that whatever beam is used there are adequate mats under the beam during training and that practising new skills is adequately supervised. It is sometimes helpful to the coach if the gymnast wears trousers as this gives the coach something to hold on to.

The gymnast must realize that such training takes a long time. But she must also realize that, in the long run, the time will have been well spent — which takes us back to the initial practice, getting used to the beam and moving with confidence and control. Even walking must be controlled. The gymnast must concentrate on her posture, keeping her head up and her back straight. She should study pictures of well-known gymnastics stars to see how they hold themselves during beam exercises. Watch, too, the top performers in major competitions. See how they walk elegantly, with arms positioned to match their movements. The gymnast must be prepared to practise, practise and practise, if she intends to master the beam with any competence.

Once the gymnast has learned to walk on the beam and turn on her toes at the end of the beam, she can begin to practise running steps in the same manner. Rhythm and pace can be varied, once the gymnast can execute a basic run, and dance steps included. Remember to vary the turns by position of the body and by position on the beam. For example, turns can be performed while kneeling, squatting or sitting; and the gymnast can turn not just at the end of the beam but in the middle as well, proceeding backwards or forwards.

All training should include elements of a routine as specified in the *Code of Points.* Thus it is useful for the gymnast to tackle mounting and dismounting at an early stage. A good tip for learning beam mounts and dismounts is to practise them on a box horse before trying them on the beam. Two examples are the forward roll mount and the handstand mount.

Below: Training for the beam can be carried out on other equipment such as the box horse or school bench.

Full turn on one leg, free leg above 90°

Forward roll

Free forward roll

Forward roll mount. Once a gymnast has practised a forward roll on a bench, she should try jumping up from a springboard to forward roll on a box horse. She must remember to 'land' on one leg as there is no room on the beam for two.

Handstand mount. In the same way, a handstand mount can be practised. When two boxes are placed end to end, the gymnast can move from the handstand into a roll, turn or forward walkover along the tops of the boxes. The move to handstand from the springboard can be varied, too: the gymnast can straddle or pike up.

Two box horses placed end to end can be used, too, for practising dismounts such as the round off dismount.

Below: Many movements on the beam can be practised on the floor or on a bench or box horse before being transferred to the beam.

Cartwheel

Back walkover

Round off dismount. The gymnast goes through a cartwheel on the end of the beam but in the handstand position turns facing the direction of travel so that she completes the landing facing the beam.

Other examples of mounts and dismounts are given below. For the remainder of the routine, the gymnast should assemble elements as outlined in the section on composition. She will be able to perform many of these movements from her training for the floor exercise. Essential parts of the beam exercise are jumps, hops, and leaps: these should be varied and practised on the floor first. Examples of leaps are stride leaps, split leaps, stag leaps, cat leaps, scissors leaps, side straddle jumps. Many other movements in the floor exercise can be used in the gymnast's beam routine; this will depend on how well she has mastered them 'on the ground'. As with the floor exercise, the gymnast and her coach must search for a routine which is fluent in performance and heightened with original links. Once more we come back to the word *balance*. The beam demands balance in performance, balance in content.

Once the gymnast has composed her routine, she must practise it constantly. An advanced gymnast expects to spend at least an hour going over her exercise or polishing up skills which she has not yet perfected. And while on the subject of skills, there is one that the wise gymnast will not neglect — the art of falling to the floor from the height of the beam. There is always a risk of injury if the gymnast does not learn to fall properly.

Below: The dismount off the beam is the climax of the exercise and can be a spectacular movement. The sensible gymnast will not, however, tackle any dismount outside her own skills and experience.

Opposite: A steady, confident dismount is a mark of good beam routine in a competition — from club level up to international standard.

The grouping of movements on the beam for scoring purposes are:

Mounts, Leaps, Stands, Body waves, Turns, Walkover — Cartwheels, Rolls, Handstands and Dismounts.

Below are examples of elements which the gymnast will find useful in preparing a competition routine.

List of movements

Two-legged squat mount.
Straddle mount.
Straddle over mount.
Squat on mount.
Y-scale.
Arched stand.
Arabesque.
Forward body wave.

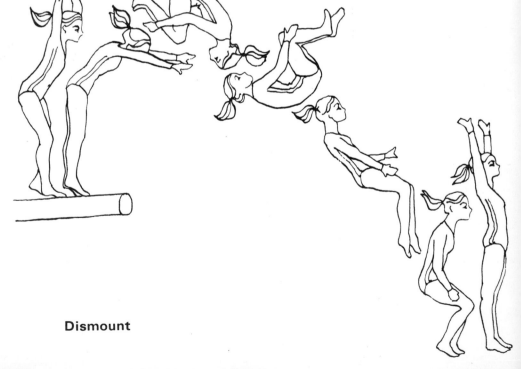

Dismount

Full turn on one leg, free leg above 90°.
Forward roll.
Backward roll.
Free forward roll.
Handstand roll.
Cartwheel.
Free cartwheel.
Back walkover.
Forward walkover.
Aerial walkover.
Handspring.
Back flip.
Back tucked somersault.
Free walkover dismount.
Handstand ¼ turn dismount.
Front somersault dismount.
Back tucked somersault dismount.

Back somersault dismount

Above: Elena Davydova, the Soviet international performer, balances in straddle support. This is a basic support position.

Opposite: Maria Filàtova demonstrates a backward walkover on the beam. This well-known Soviet gymnast has the nickname of 'Masha'.

Finally, once the gymnast has acquired confidence, poise and ability on the beam, she must remember that the beam is a medium of expression. In other words, she must perform as her true self; not as an automaton or puppet. The great performers on the beam hold their audiences spellbound not merely by agility. They project themselves so that their personalities provide the final touch in a sequence more related to art than to sport. From them, the young gymnast can learn to approach her beam routine in a relaxed and tranquil manner. It is particularly important that she does not show tension in her face. The answer is, as always in gymnastics, to be in complete control of one's movements through thorough and painstaking preparation.

CHAPTER 7

COMPETITIONS

Whether the gymnast has reached the end of her gymnastics career or has just started it, her training is intended to help her compete to the best of her ability. At club or international level, she should aim for success by understanding the challenge of competition and the tactics required to meet it.

To all enthusiastic followers of gymnastics, the great moments in the sport are seen in competitions. Be it of international standard or a small contest held by the local gym club, a gymnastics competition can promise moments of drama, excitement and sheer beauty. It is the culmination of hard and sustained effort by the competitors and their coaches.

There comes a moment in every keen gymnast's life when she is ready to enter a competition. That moment will occur when she has made careful preparations through exercises to develop suppleness, strength and stamina. She will have also learned basic skills thoroughly and have acquired confidence, poise and grace in her gymnastics performance. Only when her coach or teacher feels that the standard of her work meets that set by competitions with which the club is involved, will she be encouraged to enter the next stage of her gymnastics career — that of being a competitor.

It is very likely that the first competition in which the gymnast takes part is one held within the club. It may well be a small one, with gymnasts competing on just two pieces — the floor and vault. There are usually two

reasons for this. First, many new clubs do not have the use of all the apparatus. Second, young gymnasts will have started their basic training learning floor and vault skills. The level of competition must clearly parallel the progress of the individual gymnast. In the lower levels of gymnastics, the gymnast will compete within her own age group for obvious reasons. Some leading gymnastics clubs will hold club championships to the highest possible standards, even conducting them in the same way as international competitions. Such competitions will include, of course, all four pieces of women's apparatus.

Outside the club, the budding gymnast will probably take part in an inter-club competition. Beyond that lie area and regional competitions. In Britain, clubs are linked through the British Amateur Gymnastics Association to county and regional associations which hold their own championships. School clubs can affiliate to the English Schools' Gymnastic Association which in turn holds its own competitions. Success in a regional championship can lead to the gymnast taking part in a national championship. Perhaps the most important

Above: At the age of 14, Nadia Comaneci of Romania won the top gymnastics competition, the Olympic Games. While she won the combined exercises title, however, the Soviet Union retained the team title they had held since their entry into the Games in 1952.

127

national championship for girls in Britain is the National Development Plan which takes gymnasts through eight grades which end in the British Championshipl the Grade 1 Champion is the British Champion. Other national championships include the Lilia-White National Championships for Girls in which competitors contend on one piece of apparatus only, the British Apparatus Championships and the British Team Championships. Success for a gymnast in a major competition could mean her selection for a national squad where she would train with other talented gymnasts for possible inclusion as an international team member. This would mean visits abroad to international matches and tournaments. The most prestigious competitions in the sport are the World Championships and the Olympic Games. The former is entirely devoted to gymnastics; the latter is a battle between countries which have qualified to send teams and individual gymnasts to the Games. The World Championships are held every two years, and are now arranged preceding and following the Olympics.

The ambition of every top class gymnast is to take part in both these outstanding contests. The Olympics, particularly, gains a great deal of international television coverage, and it is through this that gymnasts become known all over the world.

There may be a wide gap in standards between club competitions and those of international gymnastics, but participants in both must have the same aims. These can be summed up as preparation, practice, performance and perfection.

Preparation. No competent gymnast ever appears in a competition without spending considerable time preparing for it. Here she will need the help of her coach or club and she will need to concentrate on many details. Some may seem obvious, but it is surprising at times how many gymnasts forget important items until the last moment. Here is an elementary check list.

1. Find out about the competition. The gymnast and her coach or teacher must be familiar with the structure of the competition, any special rules involved and, if there are sets or compulsory exercises to perform, what these are. In the case of a compulsory floor exercise, music will be involved and the club must obtain the correct tape recording. Compulsory exercises for major competitions are published well in time for gymnasts to learn them. These are usually obtained through the gymnast's national federation.

2. Enter the competition in good time. If an entry or acceptance form has to be completed and returned, make sure that this is done speedily. Certain competitions require the competitors to become members of an association such as the BAGA or ESGA. There is a small

fee for membership on an annual basis and this must be paid before the competition.

3. Check the place and time of the event. Where is the competition going to be held? When does it begin? How long will it take — an afternoon, a day, two days or more?. All these points need to be thought of and checked. Expenses will have to be considered as well. Some competitions entitle the coach and her gymnast to travelling and accommodation expenses; others do not. Care must be taken, incidentally, where payment of expenses is concerned, that there is no risk that the amateur status of the gymnast is threatened. If there is any doubt, check with the national federation.

4. All clothing and equipment must be in first-class condition. Handguards, gymnastics slippers, leotards etc. — everything the gymnast uses must be in good order. Items must be checked for wear before the competition and not at the last moment. Any item that may affect the gymnast's performance adversely must be replaced or a spare provided.

Below: Girls at Ladywell Gymnastics Club, Lewisham, prepare for vaulting practice before a club competition. Ladywell is one of the top clubs in Britain.

Practice.   Once a gymnast has found out the details of the competition, she can plan her routines accordingly. With compulsory exercises, she follows the movements laid down; with voluntary or free exercises, she and her coach must create routines that enable her to demonstrate every gymnastic and artistic talent she has. At the same time, the elements of her routines must fulfil the requirements specified by the competition rules and the *Code of Points*. Previous sections of this book have shown examples of movements needed for each apparatus and the gymnast should take care that her routines contain the correct balance of difficulty and type of element.

Having established the content of her routines (including her vaults and their numbers), the gymnast must now devote time to practising them. She must first learn them so that she can perform without hesitation, and she must also concentrate on perfecting each routine so that it becomes one continuous artistic expression. This calls for continual practice right up to the day of the competition. Great performers in other sports and arts have to do just that before they appear in public. The gymnast who does take her competition practice seriously

Below: The choice of music can make or mar a floor routine. That is why a gymnast is fortunate if she can call on the services of an understanding pianist.

has a better chance of doing well and obviously the more she puts into it, the better the results will be.

For some gymnasts, practising sets or compulsory exercises is the most tedious of activities. In a big competition, all the competitors will be performing exactly the same movements and this sense of repetition can be tedious to someone who enjoys the freedom of the voluntary exercise. Good performances in compulsory exercises, however, can make a vital difference to the result of a competition. In some major international fixtures, there is a team championship, an individual all-round competition and individual apparatus finals. In the Men's Team Championship of the 1978 World Championships, the importance of performing compulsory exercises well was dramatically proved. Favourites to win this section were the Soviet Union; their closest rivals, the Japanese, were much older. However, the 'elderly' Japanese gymnasts had learned their sets much more thoroughly than the Russians had. This fact, in the event, enabled the Japanese to clinch a narrow victory. Moral: learn your set exercises properly and do not underestimate their importance and value.

Below left: Nelli Kim talking with fellow Soviet gymnast Vassily Machuga

Below: Nelli Kim of the USSR is a formidable competitor in the floor exercise. She holds gold medals in this exercise from the 1975 European Championships and the 1976 Olympic Games.

Judges mark compulsory exercises on all four apparatus out of ten points. Deductions are usually included with the description of each exercise together with the time limit for the floor and beam exercises. If the gymnast leaves out a superior difficulty, she will be penalized 0·60 points; for omitting a medium difficulty, 0·30 points. The gymnast is allowed some freedom in the compulsory exercise in that she may reverse it totally or in part. But she may not change direction; otherwise 0·20 points will be deducted. She can also add or leave out two steps when reversing a movement on beam or floor.

The scoring for voluntary exercises, with the exception of the vault, is more complex, but it is highly important that the competitor understands it because it has a bearing on the planning of content and subsequent practice and performance. Each exercise is marked out of ten points.

Composition of exercise	5·00 points
Consisting of:	
Value of difficulties	3·00 points
Originality and value of links	1·50
Value of composition	0·50
Execution of exercise	5·00 points
Consisting of:	
Execution, amplitude	4·00
General impression	1·00
	10·00

Below: The scoreboard is unable to show that Competitor No 73 scored 10.00 on the asymmetric bars so it indicates 1.00 instead. The occasion : the 1976 Olympic Games in Montreal. The gymnast: Nadia Comaneci. The light at the top of the board signals the gymnast to start when it shines green.
The gymnast will know from a scoreboard (right) how much she has scored on an individual apparatus. But in an overall competition, she will not know her placing until the competition is over.

The gymnast can now see why equal care should be given to the way she performs her voluntary routines as well as their content. She should remember this when she undertakes training for a competition.

Examining the composition of an exercise, the scoring is based on the following factors.

Value of difficulties: 3·00 points. As stated before, the *Code of Points* requires a routine to include seven of the difficulties it lists for each apparatus, three of which have to be superior difficulties and four medium difficulties. For each superior difficulty the gymnast omits, 0·60 is deducted from her score, and for each medium difficulty she leaves out there is a 0·30 penalty.

Originality and value of links: 1·50 points. The way a gymnast moves from one element to another is a vital part of a routine, and judges look for originality from the gymnast in this area. Every gymnast should search for new and interesting ways to connect her movements; success will reward her.

Value of composition: 0·50 points. These points are awarded for the construction of the exercise. The keynote is variety; the gymnast must not be boring in her routines. She must vary her speed, the type of move, her direction. She and her coach must check that her routines are never repetitive or lacking in pace.

The execution of an exercise is very much part of its performance, so this aspect will be considered in the following section.

Below: Top Soviet gymnasts train for floor exercises by learning a group routine. This can form the basis of a display outside a competition.

Opposite: The floor exercise can be the climax of a competition. At the same time, a gymnast can enjoy its performance totally, having completed her routines on the other apparatus.

complete artistic expression and is thus worthy of a good score.

Earlier, the gymnast was asked to consider what general impression implied. In scoring, it is worth a full point. One interesting definition of general impression has been made by Carol Leidke, the American international judge, and it is worth remembering.

This category involves the ease and beauty of the movement, manner, co-ordination, poise, rhythm, radiance, security, good posture, suitability of the exercise to the girl, neatness and appearance, performance with expression, grace, dynamic movement, use of hands and head, presentation, and the overall feeling expressed by the gymnast.

When the competitive gymnast takes the trouble to create the most favourable impression she can, she will be significantly distinguished from her opponents and this will be reflected in the scores given to her by the judges.

Above: Elena Davydova is an experienced Soviet gymnast. However, she has yet to win a major world title. Here she performs a back flip on the beam.

The gymnast has four judges to impress in a big competition. These four are under the control of a master judge and are assigned to one of the apparatus. She is given the signal, usually a green light or flag, to begin her exercise by the master judge. The four judges mark the exercise out of ten points and each sends his or her score to the master judge. The master judge eliminates the highest and lowest scores, adds the middle two and averages these out to obtain the gymnast's score. For example, if the two middle scores are 9·0 and 9·2, the gymnast's score is 9·1. The master judge has to see that limits for differences in the marks are followed, as well as also producing a score for the gymnast which is used only in a dispute. Other judges, who do not mark, act either as timekeepers or ensure that gymnasts work within the limits and areas laid down for the apparatus.

During any of her routines, set or voluntary, the gymnast may fall and thus be penalized. It is therefore worth remembering the deductions set out in the *Code of Points*.

Fall from the apparatus: 0·50 points.
Fall during the dismount: 0·50 points.
Steps and hops: 0·10 to 0·20 points.
Fall on the knees: 0·50 points.
Fall on the seat: 0·50 points.
Support with one or two hands: 0·50 points.
Slight touch with one or two hands: 0·30 points.
Fall against the apparatus: 0·50 points.

If the gymnast falls at the end of the exercise and misses the dismount: 0·50 points.
If the missing dismount counts as a difficulty, there is a further deduction in the case of a superior difficulty: 0·60 points. In the case of a medium difficulty: 0·30 points.

Below: Elena Davydova forfeits 0.50 points by falling. A list of deductions which a gymnast can incur during a competition can be found in the *Code of Points*.
Opposite: Nadia Comaneci presents herself to the judges. A gymnast must do so before and after her routines.

When the day of the competition arrives, the gymnast should make sure that she is rested and relaxed. She must try not to perform in an overtired state. She should also eat lightly, with her last meal three hours before the competition. After she has reported to the competition officials, she should study the apparatus and note if they differ from those on which she has trained, or if she has more or less room to work on them than she is used to. For example, some gymnasiums have a shorter run up to the vault than others and the gymnast may have to adjust her run accordingly. She should hand in her tape recording of her music for the floor exercise to the right official. This, of course, must be marked clearly with her name. If the officials have special instructions for the competitors, the gymnast must listen clearly and follow them.

The gymnast must aim to arrive in time so that she can warm up carefully, ensuring that all her muscles are ready for competition. It is vital to warm up the body completely. The gymnast must see that her hair and her face look their best and that clothing and limbs are clean. If the gymnasium is brightly lit, a little make-up will

Below: Vera Caslavska, the famous Czech competitor, won seven Olympic gold medals and four silver. Her most outstanding achievement was at the Mexico Olympic Games in 1948 when she won four gold medals and a silver.

improve the appearance of the complexion.

Before and after each performance, the gymnast must present herself to the master judge at the apparatus. Between these two presentations, the gymnast is on her own, performing to show her love of the sport and how hard she has worked to achieve the best possible routine. If the gymnast can show the judges by expression how much she is enjoying herself, if she shows confidence and vitality, if she can demonstrate mastery of all the moves in her routine as well as prime physical preparation, then she is well on the way to becoming a first-class performer.

When a gymnast knows that she has performed well, she has the satisfaction of knowing that she has succeeded in a sport which makes many demands in time and hard effort before producing its rewards. Once a girl has been a gymnast, however, she will never lose the posture, grace and radiance which, in some ways, are the top prizes for the dedication she has shown in her aim to achieve the highest standards possible.

One highly important factor of success in gymnastics

Below: Elena Naimushina, the Soviet star from Siberia, came second to Nadia Comaneci at the *Daily Mirror* Champions All event in 1979 and received a well-deserved silver medal.

is the mental approach, first to the sport and then to competitions. A gymnast may be talented and skilled but she is hardly likely to perform well under the strain of a competition if her body and mind do not act in harmony.

So being a successful gymnast must start outside the gym, at home, at school, in whatever way of life the gymnast has. She must aim to be a 'complete' person; she must learn to enjoy every activity she does and try to make each action worthwhile. The gymnast must also learn to relax and at the same time be conscientious about matters such as grooming, eating the right food and keeping fit - all good for her morale. She must be interested at all times in the world around her and not shut herself off from the thoughts, ideas and influence of her friends, teachers and family. And as with her training, the gymnast must feel that she can improve on everything she does.

Below and opposite: While gymnastics demands total concentration from the gymnast, she must try and relax during moments when she is not working – in competition or in training. Here, three Soviet gymnasts relax during training for the 1979 *Daily Mirror* Soviet Display in London : Ilona Yarans (below) and Natalia Yurchenko and Svetlana Agapova.

When it comes to competition work, Boris Shaklin, the former Soviet Olympic star, has some good advice: *Only the gymnast who knows how to control his or her excitement and how not to go to pieces after the first failure can tackle competitions well.* What Shaklin means is that if the gymnast makes a mistake during a routine, she should carry on and complete the exercise to the best of her ability. She must not give up. She is bound to receive some kind of mark and she could score high marks on the other apparatus. In the same way, the gymnast must never be afraid of strong competition from other experienced gymnasts. She must remember that it is the final score which counts. Disregard the old saying, *for want of a nail, the battle was lost.* This does not apply in gymnastics.

The confidence of the gymnast can be boosted if she tries to experience the conditions of the competition a day or so before the actual event. For example, after warming up, she could attempt to carry out her whole competition programme with someone judging her on an

Below: Essential before every competition and training session : a gradual and thorough warm-up of the muscles. Having warmed up, the gymnast must make sure that she stays warm between her exercises.

unofficial basis. This creation of atmosphere is especially valuable when the gymnast is performing.

During the competition, the gymnast must try and relax before each piece, even if she only sits down for a moment. She should establish normal breathing and concentrate mentally on the rhythm of her routine, particularly on the performance of individual items and groups of actions. This mental concentration can be carried out at home, too. Shaklin says: *you must compose yourself for the performance of your first movements particularly carefully, because on these depends the subsequent progress of your programme. While you are performing each individual movement, give your attention not only to that, but also keep continuously in mind what comes next, so that not even the simplest movement leaves your mental control even for an instant. After all, mistakes and sometimes gross errors occur not only in the course of performing very complicated items but also in the performance of very simple ones. And this equally leads to low marks.*

Below: The gymnast should concentrate not only on performing the difficult moves of her routine but also on the simpler parts. This applies very much to the asymmetric bars. Mental concentration on routines can be carried out at home.

Above: During a competition, the gymnast is on her own. She may have the advice of her coach at hand but it is she alone who has to muster the willpower to take her through her exercises at peak performance.

Five years ago, two American scientists — Doctors Bruce Ogilvie and Thomas Tutko of California State University — isolated eleven qualities which they considered to be the most important for athletes to have to be successful in competition. These qualities are interesting in that they can help the gymnast understand herself when she is assessing strengths and weaknesses in her personality with competitions in mind.

1. **Drive.** Desire to win or be successful.
2. **Aggressiveness.** Belief that one must be aggressive to win
3. **Determination.** Willingness to practise long and hard.
4. **Guilt-proneness.** Acceptance of responsibility for actions.
5. **Leadership.** Enjoyment of role as leader.
6. **Self-confidence.** Having confidence in self and abilities.
7. **Emotional control.** Tendency not to be easily upset.
8. **Mental toughness.** Acceptance of strong criticism without feeling hurt.
9. **Coachability.** Co-operation with coaches and teachers.

Continental Sports

10. **Conscientiousness.** Possessing a sense of duty.
11. **Trust.** Acceptance of people at face value.

The gymnast and her coach can define these qualities further. There is a negative quality which is a very natural one for young gymnasts to have and that is fear. There are two sides to fear: one being related to performing on gymnastics apparatus and the other connected with the dread of performing in front of people at a competition. The former state can be lessened as the gymnast progresses in her training; the latter is again linked with experience, but needs a great deal of understanding by her coach at the time of her first competitions, to help overcome her apprehension. The gymnast must not hesitate to tell her coach if she is worried about any part of her training or competition work. One of the great benefits of gymnastics as a sport is that it helps many girls to overcome feelings of anxiety and timidity.

The gymnast must always be aware that her fellow-competitors are going through the same experience as she is. If she is mentally prepared as well as being physically prepared, she will have an advantage that will be reflected in her performances.

Above: Training and experience will help the gymnast overcome any fears about performing. She will gain confidence all the sooner with mental as well as physical preparation.

Perfection. The competing gymnast must have the determination to seek the highest standards possible and to keep to them. She must have that edge to her spirit which drives her on to improve her performances, competition after competition. She must be prepared to overcome tiredness and sometimes pain to give her best. If she does so, she will achieve tremendous satisfaction, win or lose, and, at the very least, the admiration of her coach, parents and club friends. So the first aim of the gymnast when she enters a competition is 'Nothing but the best'.

Below and opposite: Nelli Kim of the Soviet Union has always sought perfection in her gymnastics and has, at times, achieved it. At the same time, she has won the respect and admiration of fans all around the world.

GLOSSARY

AMPLITUDE Fullest extent to which a movement can be performed. Used as a standard of judging.

ARABESQUE A pose calling for balance common to dance and gymnastics. The gymnast stands on one leg with the other stretched back. One arm is extended upwards and the other arm sideways.

ARAB SPRING Also known as round-off. This is a version of the cartwheel, but is completed with the gymnast making a quarter turn from the vertical to land on her feet with her back to the direction of travel.

ASYMMETRIC BARS Second piece of apparatus in a women's gymnastics competition. Version of the men's parallel bars with the heights of the two bars varied to suit the strength of women.

BACK FLIP A back handspring.

B.A.G.A. British Amateur Gymnastics Association, the controlling body of gymnastics in Great Britain, comprised of regional associations and organizations with an interest in the sport.

BARANI A version of the aerial cartwheel or beam dismount performed without hands touching floor or beam.

BODY TENSION The control of muscles to hold the body firm without sagging during certain movements.

BRIDGE A basic movement when the body is arched backwards from a handstand with feet and hands on the floor.

CODE OF POINTS Book containing regulations governing the judging of gymnastics, published by the FIG.

BALANCE A static pose held briefly to demonstrate balance skill.

BALANCE BEAM Third piece of apparatus in a women's gymnastics competition. First developed in the last century to test balance ability. Only piece of apparatus designed simply for women.

COMPULSORY EXERCISES Also called set exercises. Published for all four pieces of apparatus before major competitions for competitors to learn and perform before the voluntary exercises.

DIFFICULTY Movement in the *Code of Points* rated as either 'medium' or 'superior'. A volun-tary exercise, apart from the vault, must have at least seven difficulties. Three of these difficulties must be 'superior', and merit 0.6 points each. Medium difficulties are worth 0.3 points.

DISLOCATION A grip on the asymmetric bars held while the gymnast hangs with her arms behind her back.

DISMOUNT The last movement in an asymmetric bars or beam exercise, when the gymnast jumps down from the apparatus.

ELEMENT A movement in an exercise.

F.I.G. Federation Internationale de Gymnastique, the world governing body of the sport. Based in Switzerland.

FLIC-FLAC A back handspring.

FLOOR EXERCISE The last exercise in a women's gymnastics competition performed on a 12m x 12m mat, involving dance, acrobatic and gymnastic movements. First women's floor exercise performed at the World Championships in 1952.

HANDGUARDS Straps made of leather, lamp wick or synthetic materials to protect the palms of the hands when performing on the asymmetric bars.

HANDSPRING A jump from feet to hands with a thrust to feet again and with the body moving in one direction.

HEADSPRING A movement where the gymnast places her head between her hands on the floor and thrusts while bringing her legs over to squat or stand.

HANG A basic position on the asymmetric bars where the gymnast hangs by her arms below a bar.

HECHT A dismount from the asymmetric bars and a vault in which the gymnast extends her arms sideways, keeping her body on an almost level plane before she lands.

HIP CIRCLE A circle around a bar in which the gymnast hold her hips close to the bar.

HORSE The item of apparatus on which gymnasts vault. In women's gymnastics, the horse is placed sideways.

JUDGE Four judges, supervised by a superior or master judge, mark gymnasts on each piece of apparatus in major competitions.

KIP Also upstart. A movement by which a gymnast

raises herself from a hang to a support position on a bar.

LAYOUT A straight and extended position of the body in vaulting, swinging or somersaulting.

LEOTARD One-piece garment worn by women gymnasts named after a nineteenth-century French acrobat.

MIXED GRIP A grip on a bar with both hands, with one palm facing the gymnast and the other facing away from her.

MODERN RHYTHMIC GYMNASTICS A recent development of Olympic gymnastics in which women perform with balls, ribbons, hoops, rope and clubs to music.

OLYMPIC GAMES The second most prestigious competition for gymnasts in the world. National teams must qualify at the previous World Championships for the limited number of places. However, the Olympics receive more television coverage and therefore more publicity than the World Championships.

PIKE A position when the gymnast folds or bends her body at the hips, keeping her legs straight.

PIROUETTE A full turn of the body when the gymnast is in a standing position.

PODIUM The raised platform or platforms in an arena where major gymnastics competitions take place and to which the gymnastics apparatus is fixed.

RADOCHLA A movement first performed by the East German gymnast Brigette Radochla which is basically a forward straddle somersault from the low bar to the high bar.

REGULAR GRIP The grip on a bar with both hands when the gymnast places her palms facing away from her.

REVERSE GRIP The palms of the hands face the gymnast when gripping the bar.

ROUND OFF See Arab spring.

ROUTINE The planned order of elements constituting a gymnast's exercise.

SALTO A full somersault without hand support.

SCORER Official at a competition who adds up the marks to find the results at the end of the competition.

SPLITS A movement, leap or pose in which the gymnast holds her legs in a straight line sideways or with either leg forwards.

SPRINGBOARD A springy piece of equipment used by gymnasts to give them greater height in vaulting or mounting apparatus.

STAG A leap or pose with one leg bent and the other held straight back.

SQUAT A movement when the gymnast bends her knees and hips while remaining upright.

STOOP When the gymnast leans forward or stoops as she vaults over the horse.

STRADDLE Basic movement when the gymnast holds her legs straight and apart.

SUPPORT A position when the gymnast supports her body on her hands with straight arms.

TSUKAHARA A well-known vault named after its Japanese originator. It is basically a cartwheel on to the horse followed by a one-and-a-half somersault off.

TRAMPETTE A small kind of trampoline used in gymnastics displays and sometimes for training.

TUCK A position in somersaulting when the knees are held to the chest.

UPRISE A swinging movement used by a gymnast to move from hang to support on the asymmetric bars.

TUMBLING A section of Sports Acrobatics which consists of somersaulting movements.

UPSTART See kip.

VAULT The opening piece in a women's gymnastics competition for which there are several kinds of vaults to perform.

VOLUNTARY EXERCISE In voluntary or free exercises, which follow compulsory exercises in a major competition, the gymnast may perform a routine of her choice provided regulations laid down by the *Code of Points* are observed.

WORLD CHAMPIONSHIPS The world's top gymnastics competition which takes place every two years. Open to all member countries of the FIG. See Olympic Games.

WORLD CUP An annual major FIG event with invited competitors from member countries.

YAMASHITA A handspring vault with the body piking before landing, and named after its Japanese inventor.

INDEX

1/7-82

Pictures supplied by:
All-Sport 6, 11, 15, 21, 33, 42, 50-51, 61, 72, 73, 80, 84-85, 88, 89,
109, 123, 124-125, 126, 127, 132, 133, 135, 138, 139, 140, 141, 148,
149
Astrid Publishing Consultants 3, 5, 16-17, 26, 27, 34-35, 43, 47, 49,
56, 58, 66, 92, 95, 104, 105, 112, 113, 122, 129, 130, 131, 142, 143,
144, endpapers
Hulton Picture Library 13 (B), 14
Mansell Collection 9, 10, 12, 13 (T)
Peter Moeller 8, 41, 67, 68-69, 83, 90, 93, 106-107, 119, 134, 136,
137, 145, 146, 147
Artwork supplied by:
Astrid Publishing Consultants